Kitchen Organization
TIPS AND SECRETS

DENIECE SCHOFIELD

BETTERWAY BOOKS
CINCINNATI, OHIO

Other fine Betterway Books are available from your local bookstore or direct
from the publisher.

00 99 98 97 96   5 4 3 2 1

Library of Congress Cataloging-in-Publication Data
Schofield, Deniece.
    Deniece Schofield's kitchen organization tips and secrets / by Deniece
Schofield.—1st ed.
        p.   cm.
    Previous version published under title: Escape from the kitchen. c1986.
    Includes index.
    ISBN 1-55870-422-1 (pbk.)
    1. Kitchens. 2. Kitchens—Planning. 3. Cookery. I. Schofield, Deniece,
    Escape from the kitchen. II. Title.
TX653.S357 1996
643'.3—dc20   96-28624
                                                                    CIP

Edited by Donna K. Collingwood
Cover designed by Angela Lennert Wilcox
Cover illustration by Kathleen Kinkopf

Betterway Books are available for sales promotions, premiums and fund-raising
use. Special editions or book excerpts can also be created to specification. For
details, contact: Special Sales Manager, F&W Publications, 1507 Dana Avenue,
Cincinnati, Ohio 45207.

TABLE OF CONTENTS

INTRODUCTION

After my wedding engagement announcement appeared in the local newspaper, I was deluged with calls from insurance salesmen, photographers, ministers, vacuum cleaner salesmen and real estate agents. I was the most popular person on the planet. One pan salesman came to the house and presented a marvelous demonstration of his wonderful (and wonderfully expensive) pans. On the cover of the brochure he gave me was a picture of a couple smiling and gazing into each other's eyes. There was another picture of the man wearing wing tips, sitting by the fireplace and petting a dog. After the salesman left, my concerned father went through the brochure with me, pointed to the pictures and told me that real life isn't like that. Good advice. Real life is more like directing air traffic at LAX (all by yourself).

It wasn't long into my marriage that I learned for myself exactly what my dad had said. There were no children, but two careers and two schedules. And two tired people at the end of the day, both with enormous appetites. We ate out a lot. Then, when the children arrived, we started going down with the ship. I was working hard all day and nothing ever seemed to get done. I was moving from one mess to another, never quite finishing anything.

Things were out of control and I turned anywhere I could for help. One of the many books I read was *About Time: A Woman's Guide to Time Management,* by Alec Mackenzie and Kay Cronkite Waldo. It said: "The woman who is concerned about managing her time more effectively must choose the kitchen as a primary target for more efficient organization." For some reason that sentence jumped right off the page and stuck in my mind.

Of course! The kitchen is a prime piece of real estate. Look at just how much goes on there: Meals are prepared and often served in the kitchen. Lunches are packed and personal effects needed for the next day are stockpiled. School work is displayed, telephone messages are taken, homework is done. Friends and family often congregate in the kitchen to visit and make plans. Food and food preparation equipment are stored. Scheduling, bill paying, letter writing . . . the kitchen is a pivotal place for home activity. The kitchen is key to effective home and time management. That, in a nutshell, is what this book is all about.

If kitchens could talk—oh, what tales they could tell! They've seen moms waking young children before dawn in order to get them dressed, fed and off to day-care. Kitchens everywhere have been abandoned during the dinner hour because of soccer practice, piano lessons, cheerleading practice—which, for some reason, always seem to be scheduled in the vicinity of the dinner hour. The kitchen has also been neglected because we're chauffeuring kids back and forth to their jobs or mercifully taking them on their paper routes. Kitchens would tell us about the single parents who are doing all this single-handedly, sometimes while working two jobs. Members of the sandwich generation are caring for their parents as well as their own children. Grandma and Grandpa have often put their retirement on hold while they sit with grandchildren during the day. There are kitchens whose masters work second and third shifts. Some of them have to work on holidays or weekends. Some of us actually want to spend more time in the kitchen—but we just don't *have* time.

My own kitchen is worthy of a tabloid feature—like the time I had to mix up five gallons of Kool-Aid. I poured all the ingredients into a big, insulated jug and had just started to mix them up when the phone rang. I hurried across the kitchen to answer the phone, not noticing that the jug's spigot was open. Sticky liquid was spewing all over the kitchen.

There was the time I fixed tacos for dinner. All I had left to do was to grate the cheese, but we didn't have any. So I unwrapped slices of American cheese and did my best to grate that.

More than once someone poured the soggy remains of their Frosted Flakes over the clean dishes I had air-drying in the sink. (It was an honest mistake; the garbage disposal was on that side of the sink.) What happened to my dreams? It wasn't supposed to be this way!

I've come a long way over the years. Besides conquering the typical on-the-job training problems—like flat meringues, dull green beans, lumpy gravy, rust in the SOS pad and all those Oreo cookies without the middles—I've authored three books: *Confessions of an Organized Homemaker, Confessions of a Happily Organized Family* and *Springing the Time Trap.* With the success of these three books, I now find myself lecturing frequently, conducting workshops and making media appearances. I wrote this book because everywhere I go, people express keen interest in this subject. They say things like:

"Our kitchen is the kind of horrible nightmare that makes you wake up in a cold sweat."

"I can spend hours cleaning the kitchen, and two minutes later it looks like the Nabisco factory after Cookie Monster was turned loose."

"My kids won't eat anything unless they've seen it sing, dance and tell jokes on TV."

"I'm too busy to cook, so we eat out most of the time."

"Every dish in my house is dirty. There is not a spot where I can even set a glass on the kitchen counter."

I'm going to put heavy emphasis on organizing your kitchen work spaces, your kitchen time and your meal preparation procedures. You may think at the outset that I'm just telling you to spend *more* time in your kitchen. That's a common complaint I hear from people before they give these methods a try. What you'll learn is how to make better use of your kitchen time so you'll be able to speed through (or eliminate) some of the mundane chores that make up KP duty. Then you'll have more time for the activities you really do enjoy.

Recently I was talking to a woman who mentioned that she had never planned a menu in her life. She said she just didn't have time, and that it was easier to just run into the store on the way home from work and pick up a few things. I've decided the excuse, "I don't have time," is a pretty poor one. Here's why. Let's suppose this woman spends an extra fifteen minutes a day stopping at the store on the way home from work. That equals one hour and fifteen minutes a week (assuming she only does this on weekdays). Planning a week's worth of menus would probably take fifteen minutes, and would allow her to go to the store once a week instead of five times. She doesn't have time to plan menus? I think I know why.

This is just one isolated example, but the same fact is borne out over and over again: Planning and organization save time.

I have taught these principles to thousands of people. Here are a few testimonials.

I was a mess. Thinking there was no hope for me I sank deeper in despair and deeper in the mess, assuming I didn't have time to get things organized. A friend gave me your book and I attended one of your workshops. Now I can see how right you were about saving time by getting organized.

One morning I had a 9 A.M. acrobics class and after the workout session I invited a few friends over for a piece of cake. (I know how stupid that sounds. You work like a fool for an hour and a half, then go home and eat cake.) I suppose I just wanted to show off.

Everyone commented on how great the house looked. "Did you get up at 4?" they asked. (I hadn't.) They were more impressed that I had not only cleaned the house, but made a cake and started dinner, too.

I'm not saying these things to brag, only to let you know that when things are planned and organized you can do everything faster and with less mental, physical and emotional stress. The rest of that day was mine to enjoy. But even on the days when I go to work (I work part-time) I have more relaxed free time than I've ever had before.

Since you showed me how to plan menus and to shop using a master list, I have saved eight hours this month. (I kept track.)

Planning and organization save time. If you don't have time to plan menus, it's probably because you're making too many last-minute dashes to the store (or the neighbor's) to pick up a few things for dinner. If you spent a few minutes planning and preparing a shopping list and went shopping once, for the next week or two you would never have to set foot in a store! That's how the woman in the last testimonial above saved eight hours.

Dovetailing is everything you promised. We've saved a fortune by eating at home! You've shown me that by dovetailing, I not only can prepare food faster, but cleanup is easier and faster, too.

(In chapter six, "Food, Menus, Meals," you'll learn all about dovetailing.)

A busy radio personality had this to say:

I tried your ideas for organizing my kitchen. I'm saving at least one hour a week by not having to look for things!

It's great. I'm anxious to try your suggestions for shopping, entertaining and meal planning so I can save even more time!

The best way to use this book, and to start realizing some of these benefits, is to read it cover to cover. Then, follow the timetable in chapter four. The timetable is only a guideline, however. You can work at your own speed, doing the job quicker or more slowly.

The book is designed so each chapter, even when used independently, helps you save time. It only follows, then, that the more of these ideas you implement and coordinate, the more time you'll save. This format is helpful, too, if you want to use the book as a future reference.

I make fun of a lot of gadgets in this book. Please, take it good-naturedly. So what if I crack jokes about your ice cream scoop (the one with the built-in defrosting element), your goose feather pastry brush or your sauerkraut forks? And whose business is it, anyway, if you save used plastic wrap and cardboard tubes? The purpose of this book is to show you how to maximize kitchen time. If you can accomplish that without tripping over your zucchini corer, your green peppercorn grinder or your sonic key finder (the "clap and your keys start beeping" variety), go right ahead and enjoy them.

Also, I put heavy emphasis on the word "you" in this book. Please interpret that to mean everyone at your house who is warm, literate (and that's optional) and breathing. The best way to save time in the kitchen (or anywhere, for that matter) is to divide up the work so no one is sentenced to hard labor.

This book doesn't take long to read. Just think—all the knowledge you need to have good food, a clean kitchen and free time (all at the same time) is just a few hours away. You can be the "Commander in Chef." Go for it and let freedom ring.

Chapter One

Time Management: The 80/20 Principle

I'm about to cut a real swath through kitchen clutter by introducing you to the 80/20 principle (first described by Vilfredo Pareto). People from economists and time consultants to salesmen and managers have applied this theory to their fields of endeavor. The 80/20 principle tells us that 80 percent of the results we achieve come from about 20 percent of our efforts.

You may have heard this idea before, but have you ever thought of applying it to your kitchen? Actually, it has a lot to do with helping you save time in that very spot!

Here are some specific adaptations: 20 percent of the items in a grocery store bring in 80 percent of the profits; 20 percent of the food you regularly purchase is used to prepare 80 percent of your meals; 20 percent of the gadgets in your kitchen help you prepare 80 percent of your meals; 20 percent of the time you spend in your kitchen brings 80 percent of the desired results; 20 percent of the storage spaces in your kitchen are accessed 80 percent of the time. Also, think about your vast cookbook and recipe collection. You probably use only 20 percent of those recipes 80 percent of the time. Of course, the 80/20 principle is an approximation, but I think you'll find it is generally accurate.

This principle really had an impact on me when I realized I could operate my kitchen very effectively with only 20 percent of the food, gadgets and recipes I kept there. And to think that I could cut down on the time I spend in my kitchen and still get 80 percent of the desired results—why, that discovery was the greatest thing since the invention of gray tube socks! Certainly I'm not suggesting that you toss out your Crockpot, the Tabasco sauce, the gravy boat and the banana split dishes. Rather, I'm suggesting that you separate the men from the boys, so to speak.

Through the course of the next few chapters, I'll show you how to decide which items fall into that high-priority 20 percent category and which are the low-payoff goods. When you identify the preeminent 20 percent of grocery items—the ones you use 80 percent of the time—imagine the hours and frustration you'll save when you learn how to never run out of those items again!

Chances are ten to one you've complained about lack of space in your kitchen: not enough drawers, no counter space, too few cupboards, etc. But when we finish prioritizing your kitchen equipment and kitchen space, you'll see how adequate your kitchen actually is. With the 80/20 principle we'll open up functional working space you never knew you had.

Whether you're operating out of a studio efficiency kitchen or one that's fit for a gourmet chef, there are four simple steps you must take to get your plan into action:

1. Discard and sort.
2. Designate work centers.
3. Prioritize your equipment and storage spaces.
4. Put the equipment into the proper centers.

Although prioritizing is the third step, I want to discuss it first to give you a basic understanding of all these principles. That way you'll have an easier time when you discard and sort, because you'll be more objective about the worth of a particular kitchen gadget. When it comes time to actually do the prioritizing, I'll be with you to show you exactly how it's done.

PRIORITIZING: GIMME AN A!

In his book *How to Get Control of Your Time and Your Life*, Alan Lakein gave the modern world the ABC method of prioritizing. Simply stated, you prioritize the things you have to do, A being the most important and C being the least important. While this method relates to time management, it also has an application to "things" management as well. (If you really think about it, we spend all of our time managing *things* anyhow!) For each category I give specific examples.

A = High Value

A's are things you use every day. It would be difficult to substitute something else for an A. Some examples of A's are salt and pepper shakers, measuring spoons and cups, stirring spoons, dishwashing detergent, aspirin and the words, "I'll fix dinner tonight"—spoken by anyone else in the family.

B = Medium Value

B's are very important. You use these things several times a week, but in a pinch you might be able to substitute something else. B's are things like refrigerator dishes, aluminum foil, a potato masher, a slotted spoon, peanut butter and jelly.

C = Low Value

C's have some value, albeit limited. These things might come in handy someday. Just as soon as you get rid of a C, you might wish to have it back. However, one of the most important things you'll read in this book is: Clutter makes everything take longer. Think about that. Everything you do every day takes longer because of clutter. We have just entered the clutter category. C's are things like a cake pan shaped like a rocking horse, corn-on-the-cob holders, olive spears, the egg piercer, the egg separator, the chestnut roaster, the cheese cuber and the set of six stainless steel lobster scoop forks.

I like corn on the cob just as much as the next guy, but that one piece of produce is responsible for an awful lot of junk: corn-on-the-cob dishes, corn-on-the cob kernel removers, corn-on-the-cob holders, corn-on-the-cob butterers. When you think how often you actually eat corn on the cob you can see the futility of keeping all this plunder stored, moved, cleaned, inventoried and replaced.

D = Total Waste

I would like to add another category of things that are always prevalent in the kitchen: D = Total Waste. These things are a total waste of time, space and money. For example: plastic lids that don't fit anything, "girlie" ice cube molds, brown paper bags filled with brown paper bags and a "Do Not Immerse" electric anything.

As you go through the discard-and-sort process that I'll describe in a minute, keep the ABCD prioritizing system in mind. Continually ask yourself: Is this gadget or foodstuff vital? Do I use it 80 percent of the time? Is it worth storing in a prime, high-priority area? Do I frequently move it to get to other, more important things? What would happen if I got rid of this or removed it from the kitchen?

A's contribute daily to what you want most—good, nourishing food served in a tidy kitchen. Keep your focus on that priority 20 percent where the highest payoff is. You should never have to move anything to get to or to put away an A.

If you've ever been hit on the head by a falling bag of powdered sugar; if you have three opened boxes of baking soda sitting around; if you're beginning to have symptoms of claustrophobia—or any other phobia—while working in your kitchen; I think it's safe to say you've got too many C's and D's sitting in, under, around and throughout your kitchen. Those C's and D's bury the A's and B's, wasting large amounts of your time, energy and money.

One of the biggest mistakes people make with organizing is that they have handy, easy-to-reach places to put things but they fill up those places with C's. Then they start complaining that they don't have enough space. The next time you catch yourself wishing for more space, ask yourself, "Are there any C's in here?" I'll bet you'll be able to uncover a whole bunch of them. So, get those C's out of your way.

Any C's you've decided to keep should be stored in places that are a little awkward to reach: high or low shelves, behind things, in another room, boxed up in the basement. These things are great candidates for your next garage sale.

The more feckless junk you have in your kitchen the more time you have to spend doing even a simple task. Let's say you want to stir a pot of bubbling spaghetti sauce. In your quest for a wooden spoon you have to dig with the determination of an archaeologist. Wouldn't it be easier to get rid of some of the junk, e.g., the bent beater from the electric mixer? (You know, the one that chewed up a spatula when the mixer was turned on high.) And why hang on to those spoons that were gnawed in the garbage disposal? In addition to the clutter, you rip up the corners of your mouth every time you try to eat with one of them. Then there are the bottles of vitamins, the three-volume set of *Eggplant*

Cookery, and the once-shiny cookie sheets that now look like the dark side of the moon in both color and texture.

Every time you need something important and useful you have to move all this junk just to get to it. Remember the sentence, "Clutter makes everything take longer." Think about that the next time you run out of Crisco, or Pringles, or Cool Whip, or coffee, or margarine, or. . . . You'll never again have to make the decision, "Should I wash out this container and keep it, or get rid of it?"

You can open up functional areas of working and storage space for A's by reducing the number of C's and eliminating your D's. Try removing all C's and D's from your kitchen and do you know what will happen? Probably nothing. But you will experience that same feeling of relief you enjoyed the last time two of the kids went to the movies and the other two had sleepovers at someone else's house.

DISCARD AND SORT

Bag It!

The four-bag or box method is the best way to speed through any dejunking or sorting process. In a nutshell, here's how it works. Using four containers (boxes or large plastic trash bags) give each a specific function:

1. Trash (or recycle). Things that no one would want or could use, e.g., expired coupons, dead batteries, warped pans, glass measuring cups with illegible or nonexistent red writing.

2. Give away or sell. It's too good for the trash, but you don't want to keep it. These are usually C's and D's—e.g., a bunny Jell-O mold; your collection of bud vases; that ceramic teapot without a lid you were someday going to make into a centerpiece, a planter or a light fixture; the Waltons Thermos bottle you're sure some collector would die for.

3. Put Away. These are things you need to keep but not in the kitchen. Or they're C's that can easily be stored elsewhere—e.g., the Christmas elf butter mold, displaced toys, the forty-piece snack and chip dip set, empty mason jars, and the "giraffe" recipe holder your son made for you in Cub Scouts out of a clothespin, a dowel and a can filled with plaster of

Paris. You really wouldn't have to put this away, except it's being replaced by a new recipe holder he made for you in school for Mother's Day—a fork standing up in a can filled with plaster of Paris.

4. Don't know. (The pièce de résistance!) Here lie the countless C's and D's you can't live with but you're not sure you can live without: dull knives you promised yourself since your first wedding anniversary you'd have sharpened, but somehow you found it easier just to buy new knives; a state-of-the-art electric candle with a Christmas-tree light "flame" complete with Dairy Queen curlicue (ordinarily you wouldn't keep this but it was given to you as the "Room Mother of the Year" award); the salad spinner (still in its box) that has yet to take a tumble; the single-serving casserole dish that's too small for you to use now, but it's part of a matching set and it "just might come in handy" when the kids leave home.

Why Bother With Boxes?

Now, why exactly does this system work? It does three things:

1. The containers keep you from procrastinating regarding the job. With each category by your side there'll be no reason to waste time running things back and forth to other places, such as taking the pliers back to the garage, bringing folded towels to the bathroom and depositing your daughter's current events clippings into her book bag. You just stand in one spot and quickly discard and sort. Another way we procrastinate is in making those heart-rending decisions. If you find yourself fondling that pig-shaped cookie jar that belonged to your mother and you just can't decide what to do with it, place it carefully into the "I Don't Know" box. You're not going to get rid of the pig, you're just going to put it on "hold" for a while. For now, let's free up some space in your kitchen for purposes more important than storage.

2. The bags or boxes enable you to stop the project in progress without having the whole room torn up. That lets you do the job in small snatches of time, if necessary. In addition, this four-box method is especially important for a person

whose eyes are bigger than her belly, so to speak. She starts out with vim, vigor and vitality, but halfway through the project, somewhat comatose, she poops out, weary, weather-beaten, worn, woebegone and wretched.

3. Since you never leave the kitchen, you won't be sidetracked by the TV, the afghan you're working on, the magazine that just arrived in the mail, or interruptions by other family members. Why interruptions? If you're like me, when buried in a project, especially a kitchen cleaning job, there's nary a soul for miles around. Seems like everyone steers clear of the undertaking for fear I'll try to round up a fledgling crew. But, if I leave the kitchen or even raise my head for a flash second, everyone thinks I'm fair game. "Will you make me a sandwich?" (Said as if auditioning for a "Read This and Cry" ad.) "Mom, I don't have anything to wear," spoken in the woeful tones of an abandoned child. And my favorite, "Mom, Jeff's bugging me." What I wouldn't give for a black-and-white striped shirt and a loud whistle.

The four boxes keep you somewhat isolated and help you concentrate your efforts on the task at hand.

As you dejunk your kitchen, remember to place heavy emphasis on identifying those A's and B's. Kitchen space is much too valuable, especially in terms of time, to waste it storing a bunch of C's and D's.

At a Tupperware party a while back, one of the guests was protesting that she just couldn't buy any more Tupperware because she had no more room to store it. The wise Tupperware lady simply said, "Tupperware is made to be used, not stored."

The same goes for kitchen spaces, especially the handy spots. If your kitchen is tiny, you may only have room for the A's and a few B's. (That's okay—you'll still be able to get that 80 percent result.) With more room you can store A's, B's and C's. No matter the size of your kitchen, though, I always recommend eliminating all D's. They waste your time, energy and money. These should be tossed out or recycled.

PICK YOUR M.O.

Now that you're a convert to the system, here are some methods (sort of variations on the theme) to help you unclutter your kitchen. Depending upon your personality, you can choose the "fast fix" method, the "party" method or several tempting alternatives in between.

Fast Fix

This procedure is best for those folks who find themselves knee-deep in the shallow spots. Sometimes the mess gets so bad, it's hard to continue functioning. Granted, this is only a temporary solution. It will cure the symptoms, but eventually you'll have to deal with the cause.

Here's how it works: You'll need some large plastic trash bags or cardboard cartons; two large, clean plastic wastebaskets; and a container for trash and/or recycling. Moving along one wall at a time, deposit everything into the trash bags or cartons. Place dishes, silverware, glasses, gadgets, etc., in one of the large plastic wastebaskets. Any recognizable and fresh-smelling food goes in the other plastic wastebasket.

Use the trash/recycle container sparingly at this point, however. Toss in only obvious pieces of garbage or recyclables, i.e., crumpled pieces of paper; soiled napkins; hard, dried-up doughnuts; empty cans; etc. Do not—I repeat, *do not*—look for garbage. Don't look through old magazines deciding whether or not to discard them; don't eye every scrap of paper to discover its value or lack thereof. If you happen to stumble across something that shouts, "I am trash," then toss it in the wastebasket. The object is to clear the area quickly.

Yes, this is going to make things hard to find, but they were probably buried anyway. Put the container of dishes on the floor by the sink, or in a corner somewhere, put away the food, throw out the trash, and put the remaining bags or cartons in an out-of-the-way spot.

When time permits, wash the dishes. Then, using snatches of time if necessary, sit down with each of the bags and go through it using the four-box method.

If clutter is interfering with your ability to function, then this system may be just what you need. It's quick and easy, and there's no turning back once it's done. It forces you into action.

Toss-It, Move-It

This is simply the four-container method taken one box at a time. It's sort of a nit-picking way to eliminate your clutter— slow, but great for people who don't have large blocks of time in which to work at home. Start with a trash basket, and just wander around the kitchen, poking through drawers, shelves and cupboards, pulling out only those things you want to discard. When the discarding is completed, do the same thing again, pulling out things that don't belong. Several days later you're ready to repeat the process, ferreting out the stuff you want to sell or give away. Continue in this manner until the job is completed.

Tidbit

The tidbit method is ideal for those who can't stand to be in a mess for long or who have a tendency to give out before the job is finished. Using the basic four small containers, you simply go through the kitchen one shelf at a time, one drawer at a time, one corner at a time. This, too, can be slow, but it breaks the job down into bite-sized pieces.

Prove It

This is an interesting method, to say the least, and works extremely well in the kitchen. All you do is box up everything in a given closet, cupboard or drawer. Put a date on the container. As you need things, you pilfer them from the box and put them away. Whatever remains in the box after six months is given away, sold or discarded. (I know a family who does this on a regular basis. They swear by it!)

Pile It

This method is beloved of children, and isn't actually a way to get rid of the mess, but it helps you live with the mess while you're working on it. All you do is make piles. Articles of clothing, linens, etc., go in one pile or area, papers and books in another, food products in another and dishes in another. Then attack each pile with the four-container method. This may be all the impetus you'll need to get started on your clutter reduction program.

Let's Party!

The party method is perfect for those who can't part with anything. Do it with a friend or friends. It's much easier to get rid of things when you've got someone encouraging you, particularly if she has a devil-may-care attitude. She can help you decide about the value of certain items.

"An electric caramelizer?" your friend asks. "Well, who knows," you reply, "someday I just might want to make crème brûlèe." With no better defense than "someday I might," your own words (if not your friend's arguments) should convince you that the electric caramelizer is at best a C, probably a D. Besides, if you make crème brûlèe at home, what new and exotic dish will you order when you go out to eat?

Since many of us curry the approval of others, friends can sometimes embarrass us into parting with stuff. When Mary uncovers your novelty cake pan collection (you know, the ones shaped like Yogi Bear, Winston Churchill and a lunar landing module) and wonders out loud if you're brain dead, of course you'll part with them. Or, maybe you'll concede to storing them in a less functional area. (Thank heaven Mary didn't see the fifteen-piece piano pan set complete with piano bench and candelabrum!)

Whichever method you choose, do it with the zeal of a gladiator. Initially you may experience feelings and thoughts like: "As soon as I get rid of that battery-operated self-stirring saucepan, I'll break my arm or something. Then I'll wish I had it back." It's OK to feel that way. I'm sure gladiators were scared, too. But that didn't stop them.

Getting things prioritized and discarded has a cathartic effect. Pretty soon your cold feet will warm up as you discover how fast you can find things and put them away. You won't dread cooking so much and you'll likely plan more thoughtful, and thus, more nutritious, appealing meals. Trust me on this one. Get rid of your beechwood lemon reamer, your English muffin breaker and your baked potato puffer, and see if I'm not a woman of my word!

Chapter Two

Creative Kitchen Storage Ideas

I f Fred and Ginger were in search of the perfect dip, could they find it in your refrigerator? Oh, sure, they could probably find it, but could they find it without spilling leftover glasses of milk, without discovering anything gray and furry and without doing bodily harm?

When you open a cupboard door do you experience the sensation of releasing a sluice gate and wish that just once the peanut butter chips, dried prunes and Oreo cookies would stay perched on that shelf or crammed in that corner?

Reaching for the bottle of vanilla, do you schlepp through sedimentary layers of two-alarm chili sauce, coriander seeds, mango paste and freeze-dried horseradish?

When you announce that you're fixing dinner, does your three-year-old ask, "What are you fixing, Mommy? Hot dogs?"

I hate to throw ants on your picnic, but even though you've discarded and sorted, keeping mostly A's and B's (and a few C's) in your kitchen, things are still a little haphazard, aren't they? (It's sort of like getting the lead in the school play and finding out you have to wear tights.) But hang in there, kid, the worst is over! Discard-and-sort was only the first step of your journey, but it was the toughest!

Referring to the previous chapter you'll see the next step (after discarding and sorting) is to designate work centers, i.e., mixing center, sink center, cooking center, serving center and refrigerator center. With these work centers in operation, all equipment and supplies needed for a certain job (or series of jobs) are organized and stored exactly where the job is done. In the following chapters, we'll set up each center and learn the specific requirements of each. But for now, let's go into some general storage basics that apply for all five work centers. That way, when it comes time to reach out and touch something, you'll have a good idea where to start.

Think about all the things in your kitchen that are frequently misplaced or missing. Stuff like: a sharpened pencil near the phone, the kitchen scissors, the plastic lid for your Stor-Savr and the chocolate chips you were going to use for Friday night's dessert.

Aside from the sheer frustration of not being able to locate something, you're wasting valuable time, energy and money on search, rescue or replacement missions. Then, there's the time- and energy-draining cross-examination, trial and conviction of the guilty party. Avoid all that waste by keeping these four storage principles in mind:

1. Store things where they are first used.
2. Store things with motions in mind.
3. Store things in well-defined, well-confined places.
4. Label things.

These four principles should be applied when arranging any work center, so let's tackle them one at a time.

POINT OF FIRST USE

Most of us, assuming that we're acting in an organized, efficient manner, put all the food in one cupboard, all the pots and pans in another and so on. We usually have a drawer or two stuffed with gadgets like the potato peeler, the nutmeg shaver, the clam opener and wooden spoons. Dishes and glassware are normally placed together in yet another cupboard.

What's wrong with that? Well, to get the roasting pan you get down on your knees and move three saucepans, the electric quiche pan, the hot dog fryer and the minicooker that french- fries one large shrimp at a time. To find the potato peeler your fingers have to do the walking (usually a marathon) to find it in the gadget drawer. You go to the pantry to get the potatoes and head back to the sink to pare them. To serve the roast you risk life, limb and the pursuit of happiness to climb up in the dish storage area to unearth the platter.

I have read many university studies that have shown how much time can be saved by a simple reorganization of equipment and supplies. One study revealed a whopping 45 percent reduction in time spent. This was all made possible by storing things where they were first used. So instead of classifying things by what they are, consider where they're used first. Now this doesn't mean that you store your Ivory liquid in the sink, but it does mean—especially if you have kids—that you store the meatballer with the Play-Doh.

Of course, things like measuring cups and measuring spoons, certain types of pans, stirring spoons, can openers, etc., are used first in more than one place. Sometimes you use an item by the sink, let's say, and sometimes in the mixing center. If you can't afford the space (or the money) to provide duplicates, simply put the item where it is most often used first.

THE MOTION IS CARRIED

Not only should you store things at the point of first use, you should also store them with motions in mind. Here's what I mean.

While I'm discarding and sorting, I get a good feel for which items are A's, which are B's and so on. (I eliminate all D's.) Those A's and B's are treated with tender loving care and are given one-motion storage. That means I can reach in and grab the paring knife, let's say, with one motion and put it back with one motion. One-motion storage is mandatory for all A's, great for B's but not necessary unless you have room, and not needed for C's.

To make one-motion storage a bit more logical, I prioritize kitchen space the same way I prioritize kitchen equipment.

Spaces for A's are always found in prime areas (between hip and eye level) and are located so you can reach in and grab things to be quickly and return them quickly, i.e., the front half of top drawers, in the front of eye-level cupboards, hip-level shelves, top shelf in the refrigerator. This is, however, your decision.

If two people work in the kitchen and one is very tall and the other is short, you have two options. One is to arrange things to be convenient for the person who does the majority of the kitchen work. Your second option is to store everything so it's more accessible for the shorter person. (It's easier to bend over than it is to get a step stool.) The ABCD method of prioritizing is both a matter of opinion and your particular circumstances.

It helps me to think of my kitchen in terms of usage and storage areas. A and B spaces are usage spaces. Don't clutter them up with C items. To get true one-motion storage, put A things in A places, B things in B places and so on. *Warning:* We're talking about an ideal arrangement, and we all know that is rarely possible. Just take care of your A's first. If there's no room for anything else, so what? You'll have 80 percent of your activities covered. Also, we'll deal with specific problems a little later.

Prioritize your kitchen space the same way you do your kitchen equipment.

You make the most from your available time and space by storing A's in convenient spots and by keeping them clean and in good repair. Sometimes it helps to have a few duplicates of important A tools, food and cleaning supplies. It isn't worthwhile to give a C (the doughnut fryer) a handy, convenient place of honor in your kitchen, unless, of course, you're the Dunkin' Donuts man (in which case it really isn't a C). On the other hand, an A deserves a reach-in-and-grab-it-quickly location.

For example, my steam canner, pectin and Ball canning book are C's most of the year. But during summer and early fall months, they move up to A's. Now, does that mean I give them A storage spots? Absolutely not. My A places are reserved only for those 20 percent of things in constant need. Their use is basically unfluctuating.

In summary:

A's = one motion.

B's = one motion (when possible), two motions, bend or stretch
    slightly.

C's = two or more motions, bend, stretch or walk; rummaging
    is OK for this category.

D's = Shame on you! A note will be sent home to the children
    of all readers who are still hanging on to D's!

DIVVY IT UP

My personal motto is (and if I could, I would print this in a
headline size newspapers normally reserve for presidential
resignations):

"Give everything a well-defined, well-confined place and always return it to that exact place."

That, ladies and gentlemen, is what this book is all about. It's
the real secret to saving time in the kitchen.

What are well-defined, well-confined places? If you were to
ask my mom for the potato masher, she'd respond with, "Top
drawer next to the sink, third compartment on the right-hand
side. It's next to the potato peeler and the paring knife." Disgust-
ing? No, no, no. It's a wonderful orchestration of kitchen efficiency. How come?

There are several reasons why giving things specific places is
important. First, when the potato masher is always in the top
drawer next to the sink, third compartment on the right-hand
side, every time you reach for it, your hand responds instinctively.
Your motions become smooth, deliberate and automatic. You can
always find the potato masher (or whatever). It is never inter-
twined and tangled with the baked potato nails, the handle of
the spatula or the gravy ladle. It is always at the ready.

Second, when things have a well-contained area to inhabit,
they stay there. There's no jostling to other parts of the drawer
when it's slammed shut. When things are compartmentalized
they become prisoners in solitary confinement, and they stay put.

Third—and highly important—if other people in the family
learn the specific places where things belong and always find
them there, they begin to have a picture in their minds: the
proper place to put something. There's only one catch: This

takes some consistency on your part.

When I first set things up, every time I opened a cupboard or drawer and found something out of place, I quickly and quietly put it back where it belonged. I decided since I was the one who wanted order and the free time to show for it, I would be the one responsible for maintaining the system, at least in the beginning. Besides, it only takes a second or two.

In the long run this practice has really paid off. The kids can put things back with the same precision I can, and they put them back where they belong. This isn't as pretentious as it sounds. Though they know where everything goes, I still have to tell the kids to put things away. And yes, sometimes I use my best town crier voice. A dash of despotism is also effective.

Finally, you know what a mess people make when they're looking for things? Well-defined, well-confined places prevent that. Again, your hand gravitates to just the spot where the desired item is stored. No muss, no fuss.

The only tools you need for this beatific state are drawer dividers and lots of them. Drawer dividers come in all different sizes and colors, and you can mix and match them so they'll fill up any size drawer. Standard drawer dividers are readily available in department, discount and variety stores, as well as large supermarkets everywhere. But aside from those typical drawer dividers, you can use anything that's square or rectangular in shape, and hollow: ice cube bins, four-sided napkin holders, liners for planters, cardboard boxes, large baby wipe containers (without the lids), baskets, dishpans (regular and restaurant-sized) and cat litter pans. Don't snicker. They are wonderful organizers and— get this—they now come in decorator colors. Drawer dividers sit on shelves to contain small bottles and packages, under sinks or on deep shelves to serve as slide-out "drawers" or trays. Drawer dividers are perfect for the refrigerator and even the junk drawer, which, by the way, is not long for this world.

LABEL, LABEL IF YOU'RE ABLE

Labeling has a lot of different applications. It can take the form of color coding. That is, yellow pencils belong in the kitchen; the kids' colored pencils go in the family room; all food marked with a red signal dot is being used as an ingredient for something this week—hands off. Or, more directly, labeling can mean actually

Use plenty of drawer dividers to give everything a well-defined, well-confined space.

listing the contents of drawers or shelves, and posting the list in or on each respective drawer or shelf so everyone knows exactly what goes where. To encourage family cooperation, many people label individual drawer dividers so Junior knows the measuring cups go here, the pancake turner there, etc. I have also labeled (with permanent felt marker or nail polish) the kitchen scissors, stapler, phone book, etc., because we have duplicates in various rooms. When things are well labeled there's never any confusion.

FOOD STORAGE

We all store food. Some of you may have a small cache—say, an extra box or two of pistachio Jell-O; water chestnuts left over from the time you didn't go through with your plans to make Mongolian beef, Szechuan style; maybe a few boxes of macaroni and cheese; and some cans of liver-flavored dog food. Still others may have enough food to operate the San Diego Zoo and feed my husband for an entire year! (Now, I'm not insinuating that Jim is an animal; let's just say that after many, many years of marriage I'm still wondering what leftovers are.)

In any event, if you're storing food on purpose or by accident, you need to do it correctly. Here are some generic guidelines that will help you when it comes time to actually set up your work centers.

The purpose of storing food correctly is to ensure the quality of the food. In other words, you want your food to be acceptable in color, flavor, odor and texture; when food is stored safely, waste is reduced and nutrition is optimum. There are several things that may affect food quality: excesses in temperature, moisture, light, time, dust and pests such as insects and rodents. Because of the temperature, moisture and light variables, we are frequently cautioned to store food in cool, dry, dark places. It's also wise to store food off the floor (two to three feet in flood-prone areas) in food-grade containers.

Many containers nowadays, including large plastic trash bags, are treated with chemicals and should not be used for food storage since the toxin may be transferred to the food. Suitable containers for food storage sometimes advertise that fact on the label. If in doubt, call or write to the container manufacturer and ask if it is approved for food use. Also, proper packaging allows for adequate ventilation and prevents condensation of moisture on packaging material.

To prevent unwanted pests, store food in clean glass, metal or heavy plastic containers with tight-fitting lids. The receptacles should have no open seams or crevices.

If you have food that has been on your shelf for an extended period of time and you're unsure of the age of the product (and thus its desirability), check if there's an expiration date printed on the product.

There are two types of codes on food packaging—open and closed. An open code is a date you can read and understand. A closed code may look something like this: CJF3113. This code can identify a number of things, like date of manufacture, batch number, time of day produced, expiration date, manufacturer's name, pull date, plant, vat number, packer, etc.

Each company has a different code and you need a key to be able to read it. While most companies probably won't send you their code key, they will tell you about the quality of a coded product.

Let's say you're wondering if those cans of creamed corn are still worth eating, or if the labels themselves would actually taste better and be more nutritious. If you write to the manufacturer (the address is on the package), give the code (usually found on the bottom). They'll write back and give you the information you requested.

If you want to learn the codes used in your supermarket, ask the employees or the store manager. Most of them have access to a master code to help them interpret the letters and numbers found on the products they sell.

There are also shelf-life charts you can refer to. Check your cookbooks, local school's home economics department and the USDA. This, of course, is only practical if you can remember approximately when the food was purchased. Never taste anything you suspect may be tainted. Sometimes toxic food tastes and smells perfectly fine. Also, any suspected food you discard should be wrapped securely so animals won't be harmed by it.

STORAGE BASICS

Keep the following points in mind:

- Avoid storing food in opened containers.
- Clean up spills immediately. Wipe containers before storing on the shelf or in the refrigerator. (Do this after every use.)
- Household chemicals should not be stored near food. Some chemicals may affect flavor and odor of food.
- Don't store foods in cupboards where pipes are located. Condensation or leakage from the pipes can damage food. Also, small openings around pipes are very attractive to insects and rodents.
- Seal all openings (such as those around pipes) with caulking, or stuff steel wool in them and cover securely with duct tape.
- When placing food on shelves or in the refrigerator, store the newest food in back so the oldest item is used first.
- Canned foods should not be stored near the stove, radiator or anything damp. Once opened, canned food should be transferred into a covered glass or plastic container and placed in the refrigerator.
- Food should not be stored near heat sources such as freezers, furnaces and hot water heaters.

The USDA also makes these recommendations (especially for long-term storage items):

1. Take an inventory and keep it current. (I'll show you how, later.)
2. Make sure food is being rotated. (Use oldest food first.)

3. Throw away any leaking or bulging cans and unsealed packages.
4. Check bulk grains periodically for rodent or insect infestation.
5. Monitor the temperature in the refrigerator (34–40° F), the freezer (below 0° F) and the storage area (average temperature should be above 32° F and below 70° F).

According to *Food Storage*, a booklet put together by the Utah State University extension service: "The lower the temperature, the longer the shelf life. Persons storing foods in a garage at an average temperature of 90° F should expect a shelf life less than half of what could be obtained in a cool basement at 60° to 70° F."

Should you want further information about storing food safely, a good source is the USDA. Another is your local cooperative extension service. If you have a university nearby, call and ask if they have an extension office in your vicinity. They work in tandem with the USDA and can supply you with information pertinent to your particular climate, growing season, native pests, etc.

It makes no difference what type of native pests you're dealing with—roaches, weevils, mice or inmates who drop things at the point of last use. You are on the way to having a user-friendly kitchen.

Chapter Three

Making Your Kitchen Accessible

Did you know you can train for a marathon right in your kitchen? That's right! A marathon, or a twenty-six-mile race. The average family cook walks about four-and-a-half marathons a year just fixing dinner! If you'd like to save your training for the great outdoors (and have more time to do it) I'm about to knock off about forty miles from your current kitchen marathon training. This is made possible by organizing work centers that provide you with storage at the point of first use—and you don't need a kitchen large enough to harbor a small aircraft. Setting up only three areas will be more than adequate: sink center, cooking center and mixing center. You can also add a serving and refrigerator center, or these can easily be incorporated into the other three.

When reading through the following lists of items for each center, remember that they are merely guidelines, to give you a starting point when it comes time to actually set up each center. So, think for yourself. For example, the serving center list includes the toaster. We keep ours in the mixing center because I fix toast while I'm frying bacon and eggs. Also, I am not suggesting via these lists that you need all these pieces of equipment. I own maybe one-third of this stuff and we're still alive.

THE SINK CENTER

The sink center is where you wash food, dispose of garbage, clean up dishes and get water for cooking. Here's a list of items often used first at the sink:

apple corer	bandages
aprons	can opener

canned soups (may also be stored in cooking center)

cleaning supplies (take necessary precautions)

coffee

coffeemaker

colander

cutlery

cutting board

dish cloths and towels

dish detergent

dish drainer, dishpan

dishes (unless stored in serving center)

double boiler (bottom only)

dried peas, beans, etc.

drinking glasses (some)

fruit juicer

funnel

garbage container and liners

hand lotion

hand soap

immersion coil

kitchen scissors

liquid measuring cup, 1 quart

measuring cups and spoons

medicines (take necessary precautions)

melon ball cutter

onions

pans (those you usually add water to first)

pan scourer

paper bags (if used to line wastebasket)

paper towels

paring knives

pet food (that requires the addition of water)

pitchers

plant food and watering container

plate scraper

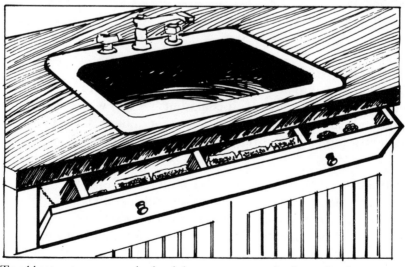

To add extra storage space in the sink center, convert the decorative front panel into a tilt-out storage bin.

potatoes
rubber gloves
silverware (unless stored in
  the serving center)

tea kettle
vegetable brush
vegetable peeler
vitamins

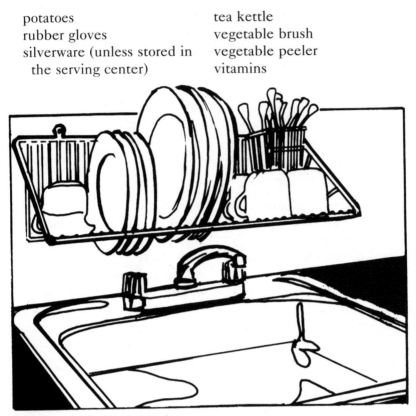

An over-the-sink dish drainer frees up counter space.

THE COOKING CENTER

You don't need to be a card-carrying genius to figure out that the cooking center is where you cook, but it's also where you store pots and pans, stir food and test foods for doneness. Here's a list of items normally used first at the cooking center:

aluminum foil
baster
broiler pan
cake testing tool
canned foods (poured
  directly into pan on stove)
canned vegetables
can opener

chafing dish
condiments
  (nonrefrigerated)
cooked cereals
cooking forks and spoons
cooling racks
cutting board
deep fat fryer

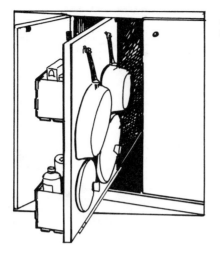

A slide-out pan rack provides one-motion storage.

double boiler (top only)
egg poacher (or store in sink center)
fire extinguisher
flour (for thickening gravy or coating meat or fish)
frying pans and covers
garlic press
griddle
ladle
long-handled fork and spoon
measuring cups and spoons
microwave oven
oil
pancake turner
pasta
plastic wrap
potato masher (or store in mixing center)
pot holders
pressure cooker

rice
roasting pan and cover
salt and pepper
saucepans and lids
seasoning mixes (poured directly into pan on stove)
serving dishes
serving trays, platters
slotted spoons
spices (poured directly into pan on stove)
stirring spoons
tea (or store in sink center)
thermometers (meat, deep fat, candy)
timer
tongs
trivets (or hot pads to set hot dishes on)
wax paper
wire whip

THE MIXING CENTER

The mixing center is simply a preparation area where you get things ready to cook and eat. You mix, blend, beat, chop, stir and

A simple wooden rack built on the end of a bank of cupboards is handy for small items.

combine ingredients in the mixing center, and since so much goes on here, you need a wide variety of tools, equipment and food. Here's a list of mixing center ingredients:

baking powder
baking sheets and pans
baking soda
biscuit mix
blender
bottle opener
bread pans
brown sugar
cake decorating equipment
cake mixes
cake pans
canisters
canned goods (not placed
   directly into pan on stove)

can opener
casserole dishes
chocolate
cocoa
cookbooks
cooling racks (or store in
   cooking center)
cornstarch
custard cups
cutters for biscuits and
   cookies
cutting board
dough scraper and cutter
egg beater

flavorings
flour and sifter
food grinder
food processor
freezer supplies (cartons,
  foil, freezer tape, marker)
garbage container and liners
  (nice to have one close
  while preparing food)
graters
herbs
jams, jellies
jar scraper
Jell-O molds
knives and sharpener
lunch boxes and Thermos
  bottles
mallet
measuring cups and spoons
mixer
mixing bowls
molds (custard cups,
  ramekins, pudding
  steamers)
muffin pans
nonpareils
nuts (long-term storage
  should be in the freezer)
pancake mix
paper towels
parchment paper
pastry blender
pastry brush
pastry cloth
pastry tube

peanut butter
pie pans
plastic bags
plastic wrap
poultry shears
powdered milk
powdered sugar
prepared mixes
pudding pans
raisins
ricer
rolling pin
rubber scrapers
salad oil
salt and pepper
sandwich bags
scale
scissors
scoops
seasoning mixes (not placed
  directly into pan on stove)
shortening
sieves
skewers
spatula (for frosting cakes)
spices (not placed directly
  into pan on stove)
spreads (nonrefrigerated)
syrup (or store in serving
  center)
tapioca
vinegar
wax paper
white sugar
wire whip

THE SERVING CENTER

The serving center is usually close to the stove, and is often combined with the cooking center. It should be handy to the eating area because its purpose is to enable you to serve meals quickly and easily. This center is optional and is probably only worthwhile in a large kitchen.

Here's a list of things to consider storing in your serving center, should you choose to have one. If not, incorporate these items into one of the other centers.

baked goods
beverages (bottled or
   canned)
bread
chips
coffee creamer
cookies
crackers
dishes*
dishpan (for transporting
   dishes to sink center)
fondue pot
glasses*
grill
jelly and jam

ladle
margarine
prepared cereals
salt and pepper
silverware*
sugar
syrup
tablecloths, placemats,
   napkins, napkin rings
table condiments
toaster
trivets
waffle iron (unless stored in
   the mixing center)

*I think it's best to store these starred items at the point of last use (the sink center) for ease in putting them away. Otherwise, if you're like me, you'll leave the dishes stacked on the counter "for now" until you have the time or the inclination to cart them back to the serving center.

A good mix is to keep the fine china, crystal, silver, etc., in the serving center and store the everyday ware at the sink center.

THE REFRIGERATOR CENTER

The refrigerator center is, of course, where foods are kept cold or frozen and leftovers are stored. But it's also where sandwiches are sometimes made, and where cold desserts are served. Here's a list of refrigerator center items:

bread
can opener
cheese slicer

covered containers for
   leftovers
cutting board

dessert toppings
freezer wrap
glasses (some)
ice bucket
ice cream dishes
ice cream scoop
jar scraper

knives
labels for frozen goods
marking pen
mixing spoons
plastic freezer bags
sandwich bags

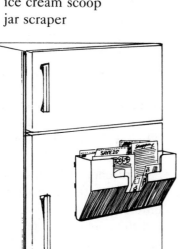

A magnetic refrigerator caddy holds everything from coupons to phone books.

In the next chapter you'll find step-by-step instructions for setting up your centers and will need to refer to these lists again. So mark these pages with a paper clip and you'll be able to flip to them quickly and frequently. In any case don't be overwhelmed. I'll also show you how to store all the trappings in a logical, efficient manner.

ON LOCATION

The locations for the refrigerator center, sink center and the cooking center are about as obvious as the Pope's religion. The sink center will be housed around the sink, the cooking center near the stove and the refrigerator center will, of course, be next to the TV. (Just seeing if you were paying attention.) Actually, though, that wouldn't be a bad idea!

The rest of this chapter will help you streamline your existing kitchen without knocking out walls, pouring cement and saying words the children shouldn't hear. But if you're getting ready to remodel or planning to build a house, chapter twelve will offer additional information.

Meanwhile, back in the kitchen, we've already located the refrigerator center, the cooking center and the sink center. Now for my personal favorite, the mixing center.

Were you to prioritize the work centers, the mixing center would be at least an A. So, it's most important to take extra pains to store things properly here even if it means a slight inconvenience to the other centers. With a carefully placed mixing center you can maximize the efficiency of any kitchen.

When I go into a kitchen, the first thing I look for is counter space. Then I check for overhead and base cupboard areas. Any span of countertop with cupboards over and under I would consider as a potential mixing center. Whenever possible, I set up the mixing center between the stove and the sink. My second choice would be next to the stove. Third choice: by the sink. Fourth choice: by the refrigerator. Last choice: totally isolated.

Here's why. When checking the centers' lists you'll notice that the mixing center, the sink center and the cooking center have many common entities. It only makes sense, then, to combine the three in order to cut down on the number of duplicates you need to store. Also, we make a lot of trips between the stove and the mixing center. So, logically you'll save a lot of time by locating the mixing center between the other two.

Combining these three has another advantage. When you want to fix a big "from scratch" meal, a casserole or a dessert, you have a full-sized mixing center to work in. Then on those nights when you want to chop vegetables for a Chinese stir-fry, let's say, you have that same available space as a full-sized cooking center. You get twice the value from your counter space because you're doubling up on storage. It's by far the best arrangement.

Failing that, my second choice would be to set up a mixing center by the stove. The mixing center and the cooking center have the most often duplicated supplies and equipment and we cover more ground between these two centers than any others. Also, most of the cooked food we prepare requires some advance preparation, again calling together the services of the mixing center and the cooking center.

The sink center and the mixing center also have a few common tools but not quite as many as the cooking and mixing centers.

Also, the sink is not used in food preparation as much as the stove is. For these reasons, this would be my third choice.

Years ago many homes were designed to combine the refrigerator and the mixing centers. But, there are few reasons to work by the refrigerator. Most refrigerated items needed for food preparation can be gathered in one trip and there are not a lot of tools and equipment needed in the refrigerator center, which forces you to have dupes in other locations as well.

Finally, if your mixing center is isolated, you will be forced to walk back and forth between centers, adding minutes and miles to your kitchen marathon.

To recap, here's a priority rundown on mixing center locations:

A = Between stove and sink
B = Next to cooking center
C + = Next to sink
C = Next to refrigerator
D = Totally isolated

Locating the serving center is more or less a matter of opinion. Ideally (a rare occurrence) it should be close to the stove, the table and the sink or dishwasher. That way you can set the table, cook, serve and clean up in a logical sequence of motions.

Now here's where opinion comes in. For years I worked in a terribly inconvenient kitchen that made that arrangement impossible, so I chose to keep the dishes, glasses and silverware by the dishwasher (to facilitate putting them away) and the serving center food items close to the table. You'll notice the food on that list requires no advance preparation. It is served exactly the way it is straight into the dishes. Also, if you're in the habit of serving food directly from the stove onto individual plates, the dishes could be stored in the cooking center.

The U-shaped kitchen always wins the time and motion studies. Because of its tight design, the centers are all concurrent and easily accessible to each other. Even so, there is no such thing as a perfect arrangement. I've worked with people who have spent thousands of dollars on their kitchens but still I hear, "I wish I had done this or that." So, don't get discouraged. While no kitchen is 100 percent, it can be pretty close most of the time.

I like the attitude of a woman who attended one of my seminars. She told me, "I'm putting a lot of your ideas to use. I'm still not perfect, but things are so much better."

My kitchen is surely not perfect, but now that it's organized correctly, it's "so much better." For example, I'm pretty much an old-fashioned cook. I cook from scratch most of the time and fix quick, family-style meals. Once in a while, I'll cook up a gourmet feast or some "continental cuisine," but most of the time it's strictly down-home style. So my kitchen is organized to satisfy that style of cooking. When I deviate from that standard, my kitchen is not quite as functional. But that's okay because 80 percent of the time it's close to perfect.

MAKING DO WITH WHAT YOU HAVE

Now, what if your mixing center is isolated and the stove has no counter space next to it? What if there are no overhead cupboards in your mixing center or by the sink? What if there's no place to set a mixing bowl after you've used it? How can you make awkward centers more functional?

If you're in dire circumstances, the first thing to do is to generously eliminate everything but those A's from your kitchen. That single effort will bring greater results than anything else.

Here are some other solutions. Let's say your mixing center is isolated from the cooking center and you can't combine the two areas. As long as you have a good mixing center, this arrangement isn't really as bad as it sounds. Here's what you do. Suppose you're making spaghetti sauce. Begin browning the meat, onions and vegetables at the cooking center. Meanwhile, at the mixing center, combine the other sauce ingredients in a mixing bowl. After the meat is brown, drain off the fat and pour the prepared sauce over the meat and simmer. In other words, prepare everything at the mixing center and carry it to the cooking center when it's ready to be cooked or baked.

A wheeled cart can be useful in all the centers, if you have space for it. Next to a stove it can hold the electric frying pan, broiler pan, aluminum foil, bouquet of utensils, saucepans and lids, fire extinguisher or any other items needed there.

It can also serve as a portable mixing center. Gather needed supplies for a particular meal and place them on the shelves of the cart; the top can serve as extra counter space. A wheeled cart can also be used as a permanent mixing center, though you'll probably have room to store A's only.

A portable mixing center can be rolled wherever it's needed.

A portable bar is another storage solution. It can serve as a kitchen island, holding cookbooks, placemats, supplies, etc. It can also be used as a buffet or to supply extra counter space. In smaller kitchens keep the bar in another room and roll it into the kitchen when you need extra work space. Or, shop for a free-standing cupboard to butt up against a wall, or use it as an island.

My sister, Judy, bought an unfinished chest of drawers for her kitchen. She painted it to match the kitchen decor so it's pretty as well as handy. The deep drawers hold bins of flour and sugar, tablecloths, placemats, baking sheets, pans, food grinder, graters, lunch boxes, etc., and the chest is low enough to lend extra counter space to the kitchen.

Stackable storage towers reconfigure easily. Choose shelf and/ or drawer units.

A baker's rack is a superb way to get extra storage space and to display collectibles, plants, books or your favorite beverages. In addition to open shelves, some racks even have drawers or lower shelves with doors.

A desk/cabinet unit with drawers, desktop and shelves can give you much-needed work space or can become a room divider. A huntboard with or without a hutch gives additional storage space and can also stage a great buffet or display.

Wooden storage towers are narrow shelf units (usually about

Stacking bin drawers provide extra storage.

twelve inches wide) that fit even cramped quarters. They come in varying heights with three, four or five shelves. Look for units with adjustable shelves and doors.

Microwave carts, free-standing cupboards, dry sinks and jelly cupboards are readily available, as are unfinished chests. They can provide you with custom-fitted storage. Armoires provide closed shelving and deep drawers (ideal for linens). A pie safe has shelves and drawers. The unfinished pieces can be painted, stained or stenciled. Decorative knobs can be added as well.

Additional counter space can also be gained by having a board fitted to span the front half of the sink. Be sure the board only goes one-half to three-quarters of the way back, so you can still use the faucet. Also, have a backstop installed under the board (a piece of wood will do) so the board won't slide around or pop out while you're working on it. A board can be hinged to a wall and lowered only when needed, or have a pullout board installed under a convenient countertop. Or, open up a drawer and put a

A fold-down table is a great space stretcher in small kitchens.

cutting board over it to give you a few more feet of working surface.

No place to set a mixing bowl once you've used it? There's no need to use precious counter space as a holding place for dirty dishes. A restaurant-sized dishpan or tall plastic wastebasket sits right on the floor by your working area or under the sink and holds dirty dishes until you're ready to wash them. (Rinse them off quickly, then place them in the holding container.) Or if you have room, a dishpan filled with soapy water sitting on the counter in your mixing center helps you clean up as you go.

If a sink isn't close to your mixing center, you can pare vegetables and fruits over newspaper or freezer wrap in the mixing center and toss the scraps away. And if you have lots of storage space by poorly placed appliances, you can opt for mini versions placed wherever you want them (i.e., toaster/oven/broiler, hot plate, electric frying pan, mini refrigerator, mini microwave, immersion coil).

If the area above your kitchen cupboards is enclosed by a soffit, you can replace the front piece with a sliding door, fabric or a small-hinged door. If no soffit is installed, you can hang a curtain from the ceiling to conceal the storage area or install drop-down doors from a piece of molding installed on the ceiling. Just be sure the cupboard can withstand the extra weight. If not, the unit should be reinforced. Of course, soffit-area storage is best reserved for C's.

Convert a soffit into C-type storage areas by installing small hinged doors on the front panel.

One friend has a filing cabinet in her kitchen. The cabinet is decorated with paint and wallpaper and provides her with a pretty storage area for appliances, cereal boxes, serving trays, large bowls and all sorts of cargo. (I suppose I wouldn't be an organizer if I didn't remind you that the most inexpensive way to get more storage space is to get rid of seldom- or never-used items.)

Standard open wooden shelves stacked up next to an unused wall provide pantry storage for food, bins, cookbooks, pans, appliances—whatever. Sometimes just changing the position of the refrigerator or the table will open up enough room to house a new countertop or a few extra shelves.

So far I've been talking in generalities, but in the next few chapters we'll get into specifics: how to store everything from the spices to the SOS pads. Once your centers are physically fit there'll be plenty of time for your own fitness program. You'll even have time for a good, brisk sit!

Chapter Four

Setting Up a Convenient Kitchen

W e live in an age of megabucks, megatrends and mega-abbreviations. We've got the NCAA (not to be confused with the NAACP); the ASPCA (not to be confused with the AARP); and there's the NFL (which, according to my husband, is not to be confused with the CFL). Wait. There's more: CEOs (who, when they're not involved with R&D are getting some R&R); CPAs (most of whom belong to the NAA); UFOs (reported to the USAF); and, lest we forget, those dreaded POSSLQs (persons of the opposite sex sharing living quarters) brought to us by the US Census Bureau. And where do POSSLQs go when they feel they've been discriminated against? To the ACLU, naturally.

Yes, over the years we've saved countless hours, millions of dollars and gallons of ink just by using abbreviations. For instance, when referring to the MTUOP as such, instead of as the Mobile Training Unit Out for Parts, you can save writing twenty-four letters or 3.783 seconds every time it comes up in a conversation. Staggering.

The purpose of abbreviations is not always brevity (with the exception, perhaps, of the ALROS or American Laryngological, Rhinological and Otological Society. The letters, I suppose, are just plain easier to remember, except perhaps, with the ASTSEC-NAVAIR or the Assistant Secretary of the Navy for Air).

If you've been confused as I have with all this jargon, maybe a little simplicity would help. I'm going to show you an abbreviated system that's so incredibly easy, all you have to do is remember three C's. These are the CCCs of setting up a work center.

C = Clean
C = Cull
C = Categorize

C-ING THE MIXING CENTER

Assuming you've done all the preliminary discarding and sorting as outlined in chapter one, you're almost ready for your first C.

But, before you slide headfirst into the base, so to speak, I want you to go in with your eyes open. We're starting with the mixing center because it's the most important center, it contains a large portion of your kitchen equipment, and it's the hardest, messiest part of your kitchen reorganization. However, setting up a good mixing center is what streamlines every task performed in your kitchen.

To make it less overwhelming I have broken down the job into manageable portions so you don't have to upend the kitchen for three-and-a-half weeks.

I'll describe the fastest method first; then, after you've read through the entire process, I'll give you a piecemeal approach. That way, if you're working away from home, if you have pre-schoolers or if you're just plain faint-hearted or even lazy, you can still reach the summit without raising dust and working up a sweat.

Even so, it would be a good idea to plan simple, quick meals for the week you're working on the mixing center. Soup, sandwiches, salads, fast foods, stuffed baked potatoes, Crockpot meals or casseroles would be good choices. Once you've made out your menus, segregate the ingredients for these forthcoming meals so they won't get lost in the shuffle.

Just promise the family pâté of pheasant supreme, asparagus brûlée and Caribbean pineapple flambé after the project is completed. Whatever you entice them with, be sure the name of at least one dish has a little mark over a vowel somewhere. That simple accent is what turns smooshed-up goose liver into pâté de foie gras. It works every time.

C = Clean

As soon as you've decided what area in your kitchen to earmark for the mixing center, clean it out. Take everything out of the designated cupboards. If possible, relocate this equipage to other cupboards or simply corral it in boxes so it's out of the way. If you suspect some of these items will be used in the mixing center, place them on an adjacent counter or nearby table.

When the area is cleared, it's time for a thorough cleaning. Wash and dry cupboard interiors, shelves and door fronts. Ditto with the drawers. Wash and dry the countertops, backsplash and mixing center wall. If desired, cover the drawers and shelves with shelf liner. Once the mixing center is clear and clean you're ready for step two.

However, if you want to call it a day, this would be a good stopping point. Yes, you'll have to rummage a little to find the things you pulled from the mixing center, but at least the whole kitchen isn't torn up.

If, in the process of cleaning, you've set aside things that will be used at the mixing center, go ahead and put them away in the clean shelves and drawers. Don't worry about organizing at this point. We're just getting things out of sight.

C = Cull

Flip back to page 29 and scan the mixing center list of suggested foods and equipment. Put a red check mark or draw a circle around any of the items you currently use. Do you use it first at the mixing center? If so, tick it off. Is there any mixing center gear you normally use that's not included on the list? If so, pencil it in the margin.

Remember, the mixing center is an A. So if you've only got one can opener, let's say, and you use it in two different locations, the mixing center wins out. It's okay to slightly inconvenience the other centers. (You can always keep the electric can opener in the mixing center and a small handheld model at the sink center.) The mixing center always has priority over the other centers.

Now, with your personalized list in front of you, cull all the items you've designated as belonging to the mixing center. Put them on the mixing center counter and put the overflow on a nearby table. You may even want to set up a card table to keep things handy.

Keep your eyes peeled for any C- and D-priority gadgets and foodstuffs you may have passed over in your discard-and-sort session, and cut your losses. These impulse purchases were a waste of money; admit it and go on. Don't let impulse dupe you again by robbing you of needed space. (This speculation is based on the assumption that no red-blooded American shopper in her right mind would actually plan to buy an electric duck plucker with revolving rubber fingers that plucks fifty-three ducks an hour.) It's time to let go and live.

Once you've rounded up all the parts—and don't forget the ones you may have stashed away in the mixing center after your cleaning session—it's time to begin step three.

C = Categorize

Step three is the most time-consuming, so let's break it down into at least two work days. To finish up your culling project, you need to categorize all the mixing center chattel into three priority piles. If you're going to wrap up your day's work after this prioritizing, it's best to use three boxes or containers, so you won't have a quagmire in the interim. And even if you do keep plugging away, I strongly suggest you put all the smaller (and nonfood) C-priority things in a box.

Again, this is based somewhat on personal caprice, but let me give you an example of how I'd prioritize things. Some A's would be: can opener, mixing bowls, paring knife, cookbooks (A's only), wooden spoons, pancake turner, tongs, measuring equipment, trash container.

Some B's would be: electric mixer, grater, aluminum foil, baking powder, food processor, salad oil, ricer.

Some C's would be: cake decorating equipment, Jell-O molds, tapioca, custard cups, mallet, skewers, sieves, chafing dish.

I think examples are important for clarity, but they can be misleading so I want to caution you again. My food processor is a B to me. If you make your own baby food, let's say, then your food processor is definitely an A.

Another caution: Be honest with yourself. Don't kid yourself into thinking something is an A because your mother gave it to you. A's are things you use more often than once a week. Without any given A you would experience a lot of inconvenience. It is hard to substitute something else for an A item. My family, for instance, loves mashed potatoes, and without a potato masher it would be difficult to get the desired results and satisfy their appetites for mashed potatoes. On the other hand, without a cake testing tool I could simply use a toothpick or a piece of uncooked spaghetti, or I could touch the center of the cake with my fingertips. In that case it's easy to improvise to do without a cake tester completely.

At the risk of straining my categorizing to the breaking point, remember:

A = vital (could hardly function without it)
B = important (inconvenient to function without it)
C = limited value or some value (could function without it if you had to)
D = complete waste (don't need it)

But if you're the type of person who carefully places the pencils pointing the same direction in the drawer; if you could serve Beef Burgundy on the top of your hot water heater at any given moment; if you iron brown paper bags before placing them in order of descending size in the paper bag caddy, you're going to have some problems with this categorizing. For you it's going to be like trying to pick out your favorite noodle at a spaghetti dinner. You're going to pick up the Bisquick and agonize over whether it's an A or B. Heaven forbid you should make a mistake and misjudge it.

If you're suffering from Manic Perfectionist's Syndrome (MPS—not to be confused with PMS), here's Plan II. All you need to do is differentiate between A's and C's. Put all the A's and B's in one category and C's in another. C's seem to be somewhat more obvious than A's and B's, thus they're easier to categorize. See if Plan II isn't just the impetus you need to keep the CCCs from becoming *zzzzzzz*'s.

Now is a good time to stop. What lies ahead is a good day's work and you'll want to be refreshed and ready to go. For the rest of the day you'll need to operate the mixing center out of the categorized boxes unless, of course, you quickly load the paraphernalia into the empty cupboards. If you opt for this method, be sure to keep everything grouped, at least, into ABC categories. Either way you'll be running the kitchen in a somewhat haphazard manner; but at least it won't look like an area worthy of being measured on the Richter scale.

C-ING IS BELIEVING

You've come a long way, baby, as they say, and now the end is in sight. What remains is my favorite part of the whole CCC process. Here's the grand finale: categorizing spaces and organizing the mixing center.

Take a close look at your mixing center and decide where all your A (or A and B) spaces are. Where will you stow C's? Again, if you're an average-sized person, A's and B's are the top two drawers in a base cupboard and front half of the top two overhead cupboards. The front half of a top base cupboard shelf would also be an A or B.

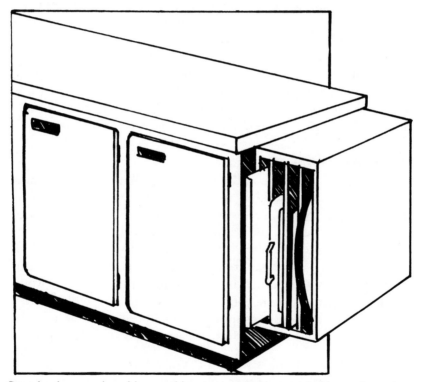

Stretch a base cupboard by attaching a tray or baking pan holder to the end.

All you have to do now is to put the A and B gadgets into A and B places and put the C things in those areas that require steps, stretches, step stools or bending to reach. It's OK to move things out of the way in order to reach them, too. It's also acceptable (and sometimes necessary) to store mixing center C's in an area other than the mixing center. The main thing is to make those A's and B's as handy as your space will allow.

If you're strapped for time, here's how to subdivide the whole CCC project. With some careful planning you can break down this clean, cull, categorize routine into micro-pieces. Naturally, it'll take longer before you realize the final result, but you'll be able to get out of the kitchen without a court order.

Here's a plan of attack: CCC the base cupboards and drawers, then CCC the overhead storage areas. Or CCC the gadgets and their storage areas, then CCC the food and its storage area.

Or try this. After you've personalized the mixing center list, adding and subtracting all the variables, prioritize the items on your list into ABC categories (or A and C categories if you're a victim of MPS). Then categorize your mixing center cupboards, drawers and shelves into ABC areas and decide which A things will go into which A spaces and so on. In other words, the mixing center will be carefully planned before you actually do anything. With such organized premeditation you'll be able to CCC one drawer at a time, one shelf at a time, one cupboard at a time.

STARTING OVER

Following the timetable at the end of this chapter, you can now organize your entire kitchen using the CCC approach. The mixing center rules you have just read are the standard CCC procedure for every center you set up. Just substitute "sink center" or "cooking center" where "mixing center" appears. Should you have enough kitchen space or a particular need for a refrigerator center or a serving center, you may include those areas as well.

The biggest problem you're likely to uncover will be with food. If you have reserve supplies, it will be impossible to store it all in the various centers. In that case, there are a few options.

- Keep just a week's worth of supplies or your "use all the time" staples (whatever your space permits) in the centers and the rest in the pantry, a less convenient cupboard or other storage area.
- After you do your shopping, place the food required for the week's menus in the various centers and store the other items in a separate location.
- Some people like to shop at home. Here's what I mean: If

you've got a freezer full of meat, fruits and vegetables, and a pantry stocked with canned, bottled and boxed goods, you can plan your menus for a week or two and pull all the necessary food items from their storage areas. Then store them for your immediate convenience in the various centers.

- If you have a pantry or large chef's cupboard where a stock-pile of food and other supplies is kept, it's best not to include this area when you CCC. After you've CCC'd the gadgets and other equipment for each center, see if there's enough room for at least the A food items, and pull those things from the pantry.

Remember that the ideal is seldom a reality. To some degree you are bound by the physical structure of your kitchen. But aside from what appears to be an architectural plot against us, we can alter, to some degree at least, the speed and efficiency of KP duty.

I have taught this concept to thousands of women and some men too. They have come up with very helpful and practical solutions, especially when elbow room is pretty much restricted to the periphery of the ribs.

One woman went so far as to categorize her spices: cinnamon, oregano and chili powder were A's. Saffron, turmeric and fenugreek were C's. So she alphabetized the A's and put them in the front of her spice drawer and put the C's in a less handy location. This left a lot of room in the drawer for more important and oft-needed items.

Another woman made homemade suckers about every three months or so and her mixing center was crammed with specialty bottles of flavorings, molds, sucker sticks, labels, wrappers, etc. When she removed all this stuff and put it into a C location, she made her mixing center not only more spacious but much more functional on a day-to-day basis.

Like many folks, I have a bouquet of tools sitting in a crock on the counter of my cooking center. It holds the wire whip, wooden spoons and spatulas I use every single day, items for which one-motion storage is vital. Also, this crock arrangement frees up already limited drawer space.

An ambitious mother of three converted her front hall closet

Fliptop cupboard doors over the refrigerator make the contents more accessible. A basket provides extra storage.

into a pantry complete with adjustable shelves. She had considered the closet a C because it was always used to stash junk. And, when guests came over, all their coats were put on someone's bed, anyway. So by converting the space into a food storage area—which, by the way, was only a few feet from the kitchen— she gained several square feet of B- and C-type storage.

ON THE LOOKOUT

If your new kitchen system is a drastic change from your old method, give it a chance to work. You may experience a little frustration for a week or two until you feel comfortable with the locations of your necessities. Keep working with it and you'll begin to see how quickly and easily you can accomplish kitchen chores.

If, however, you notice snags in a particular and often repeated operation, say making waffles, salad or sandwiches, see if you can determine why the snafu is occurring. Here's a checklist of possible causes:

1. Are things being stored at the point of (most often) first use?
2. If so, do you need duplicates? Dupes are especially helpful when centers are several steps away from each other or totally isolated. Space permitting, it's usually wise to have twins of measuring spoons and cups, can/bottle openers, stirring spoons, pancake turners, mixing bowls and salt and pepper shakers.
3. Do cupboards, drawer dividers, shelves or gadgets need to be labeled? This can save hours of nagging and keeps you from having to remember where everything is supposed to go. (Actually, it's probably a good idea to label where everything goes until everyone is familiar with the new setup.)
4. Did you categorize something as a C or D that is actually a B?

Be mindful of sets of things. You may have a set of casserole dishes or mixing bowls. Are all the parts of the set the same priority? For about fifteen years we had a set of mixing bowls sitting on the shelf. Because of the size of our family and the amount of food I fixed, I rarely used the small one. But that bowl was moved two or three times a day so I could reach the middle-sized bowl and the large bowl. Finally it dawned on me that the little bowl was a C and I moved it to a C location and got it out of my way once and for all.

I did the same thing with my vast cookbook collection. I kept in the kitchen only those cookbooks that I use and refer to frequently. The rest of the books were put in the other room on the bookshelf.

If you've ever tried to fix your own plumbing, tune up the car or get the garage door back in the track, you know that it takes three-and-a-half hours longer than if a professional were to handle the job. (Not to mention the hefty increase in cash outlay for emergency room charges!) Aside from more experience and perhaps know-how, the pros have the tools to do the job. If we had the specialty equipment Mr. Goodwrench has, we could rotate the tires in twelve minutes, too.

My point is this: It's possible to pare down your belongings to the point of gross inconvenience.

When I first got my food mixer/processor/blender I decided, purely for aesthetics, not to keep it on the kitchen counter. The only other available place was down the hall in the linen closet. Surely, I thought, I'd have enough self-discipline coupled with the desire to use my new toy to walk down the hall and cart it to the kitchen whenever I had a need for it. *Wrong!* Every time I had to grate, knead or blend something I'd just say to myself, "It's easier to do it by hand than it is to lug that food processor into the kitchen." Within two weeks, after I realized my error, the machine was sitting in a corner on the counter.

While it is smart to rid your counters of all unnecessary apparatus and decorations, be sure you don't do it to a point where things become awkward and more difficult than they need to be.

Here's an approximate timetable to follow, set up to guide you through a complete kitchen overhaul in just three or four weeks. Sure, you can work at it faster if you have the endurance of a weight lifter, the determination of a black belt bargain hunter and the patience of a Slurpee clerk at the 7-11. On the other hand, if you work outside the home, if you've got preschoolers, or if you just plain can't stand the thought of the undertaking (pun intended), give yourself two weeks for each designated week.

TIMETABLE

WEEK ONE

Monday	Plan simple menus for at least two weeks. Shop for ingredients. Group nonperishables in a box or other central location. Do whatever advance food preparation is possible for this week's menus (i.e., brown hamburger and freeze in serving portions, mix meatloaf or form meatballs and freeze, grate cheese, set a salad, make up a spice mix, etc.).
Tuesday-Saturday	Discard and sort. Go through entire kitchen using the four-box method.
Sunday	Your day off.

WEEK TWO

Monday	Plan location of mixing center, cooking center and sink center. Again, do whatever advance food preparation is possible for this week's menus.

Tuesday-Saturday	CCC the mixing center.
Sunday	Your day off.

WEEK THREE _____

Monday	CCC the cooking center, sink center and clean the re-frigerator (if you're not setting up a refrigerator center).
Sunday	Your day off.

WEEK FOUR _____

Monday-Saturday	CCC the refrigerator center and the serving center.

Finished! Convenient kitchen realized!

Chapter Five

Organizing Drawers and Cupboards

I f reading the foregoing chapter made you feel like you've just gone nine rounds with Mike Tyson and you haven't the strength for even one quick uppercut, don't give up and toss your sweat socks into the ring. The hard part is over and before long, you'll be declared the official winner.

Now that you've soaked up the knowledge and you're familiar with the plan, you're ready for some high-powered ideas that will wreak the final blow. Once and for all let's put an end to kitchen waste: wasted time, wasted space and wasted energy (yours, in particular).

If you're working in a severely cramped or poorly designed kitchen, you may have to summon up some creativity to help you get the job done.

Here's what I mean. We are all bound to some degree by the architecture of our kitchens. For example, the measuring spoons, rubber spatula, gravy ladle and potato peeler may seem best suited to drawer storage, but when you have no drawer space, start using your imagination.

Here's how: Think of the four storage options. No matter how commodious or circumscribed your kitchen, there are only four ways to store things: hang them up, store them in a drawer, set them on a shelf or put them on the floor.

So, if drawer storage is not possible, ask yourself if those tools can be hung up, put on a shelf or stored on the floor.

Whatever storage problem you face, you can find your best storage option by looking at these four possibilities. Frequently, you can work around the existing architecture of your kitchen and save the many hours and dollars of a remodeling project.

Take a trip to the nearest home improvement center or dis-

No drawers for silverware? Store it on a shelf or countertop.

Make a simple knife rack out of scrap wood and attach it to a wall or cupboard base.

count store and check out the wide variety of organizing imple-
ments and units they have now. You can purchase closet organizing systems you can install yourself that will effectively help you
utilize every square inch of available space. Things from vacuums
with on-board attachments to gadgets that hang up the iron and
ironing board save you space and get you organized.

What can you hang up? Mops, brooms, ironing boards, vacuum
hoses, bags of attachments, spice racks, pocketed shoe bags to
hold cans of cleaners, pails of supplies, pots and pans, cooking
tools, and knives (on a magnetic holder or wooden form). Even
bags of food like potato chips, powdered sugar and marshmallows
can be hung up. Just fold over the end of the bag, clamp it shut
with a spring paper clamp, and hang it up. You can also hang
placemats using a spring action clamp (or even a clipboard).

Keep knives and scissors within easy reach with a magnetic rack.

Your garbage can hang up, too, by using a garbage bag caddy. This organizer attaches to the inside of a sink cabinet door and is made to hold either plain paper bags or plastic trash bags. There are also hanging racks made to hold paper sacks and boxes of foil and plastic wrap.

Want your trash easy to reach and out of sight? Hang a garbage bag caddy inside a cupboard door.

Pan racks, mounted underneath a deep shelf, slide out to reveal hooks on which to hang pots and pans. Cups, mugs, measuring equipment and any number of gadgets can likewise be hung on revolving or slide-out cup racks. Black wrought-iron pan racks are easily installed on a bit of wall or ceiling space.

Where can you hang things? On a wall, inside a cupboard or closet door, high under a sink, on a grid or pegboard, behind a door or on any sturdy, vertical surface. Screw-in and self-adhesive hooks come in varying sizes and strengths, enabling you to hang things just about anywhere.

Grids are widely available, or you can make your own. You will need ten 1″ × 2″ pieces of wood. (The length of the wood pieces depends on the size you want the finished grids to be.) Place two vertical slats on your work area. (The distance between the two slats will be the length of the horizontal piece.) Place the remaining vertical slat midway between. Now, beginning at the top, place the horizontal slats so as to form seven equidistant rows. Nail slats in place, paint and hang equipment on slats with *S* hooks. (Lattice or pegboard are other possibilities.)

Another hanging grid is made by simply attaching a piece of

A grid hanging in the cooking or mixing center provides one-motion storage (especially handy when drawer space is limited).

latticework to the wall or ceiling.

Don't have enough shelf space? If you'd like more, open your cupboards and look for "head space." Are there areas where you can see the back wall of the cupboard? This usually occurs when you have something sitting on a shelf that's not too tall: cups, silverware chest, serving dishes, etc. An easy solution to get more shelf space is to purchase half-shelves. These are small vinyl-dipped steel shelves that can stand on an existing shelf, thus doubling your horizontal surface. They are available at discount stores and home improvement centers.

There are also many different types of dish holders that really shrink the amount of space it takes to store your dishes. (The one I use holds the plates and bowls vertically.) There are bins that slide under and hang from an existing shelf, again utilizing wasted space. Many varieties of shelving units hang over a closet door or on the wall behind a door.

Plastic freezer containers, small sturdy cardboard boxes or small purchased racks can be tacked to the inside of cupboard doors to hold spices, envelope packets, gelatin and other light-weight items.

Look up! Shelves for seldom-used articles can be added above a door or anywhere about two feet from the ceiling. They can be made inexpensively, using particleboard supported by angle

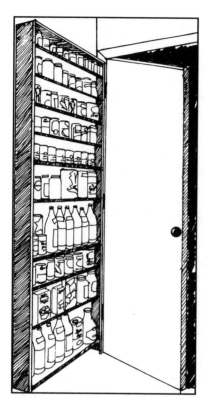

For extra storage, build a narrow shelf behind a kitchen door.

Hang a vinyl-dipped steel shelf inside a closet door.

irons. That way you can free up your cabinet space for everyday utensils in constant demand. Also, if you have two cupboards with a window or a door interrupting them, a bridge over the top of the two units provides a shelf for decorative or infrequently used things. But this is only recommended if you're in dire need of extra space. The things stored on these high shelves are hard to retrieve and the shelves themselves are difficult to clean.

For the do-it-yourselfer a hanging storage unit can be made using only a screwdriver. Standard-sized shelves (8″ × 24″ seem just the right size) made from particleboard form the shelves and uprights. Paint or stain and glue together. T-plates are positioned for support. (See illustration on page 61.)

Small shelf units can be attached to the inside of cupboard doors.

Large and small, single- and double-tiered lazy Susans are readily available and beloved by many. They waste space, so proceed with caution, but they are extremely useful in cupboards with dead corners that are hard to reach.

No drawers: Without enough drawer space, you have to rely heavily on the other storage options. But you can purchase drawers that mount (using a screwdriver) under an upper cupboard unit or under any high horizontal surface. Freestanding drawer units made from wood, metal, cardboard or plastic can supply extra drawer space. (Keep the cardboard away from fire and water.)

Dishpans, drawer dividers, ice cube bins and other shallow containers can function like a drawer if placed on a shelf and used as a slide-out tray.

Every kitchen has a floor. Do you have clean spaces between the refrigerator or stove and a base cupboard in which you can stand serving trays, a large cutting board or cookie sheets? Is there a corner where you could stand a crock, basket, stacking bins or other large containers? These can hold fruits, vegetables, flour, sugar, baking pans or just about anything.

Use your imagination, think creatively and remember those

For extra C-type storage, build a shelf over a bank of cupboards.

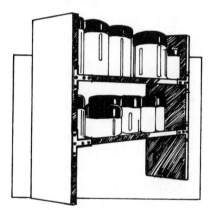

A simple, freestanding shelf made from scrap lumber and T brackets provides extra storage right where you need it.

four storage options. They may just be the magic wand that turns your kitchen from a pumpkin into a luxury liner, or if not a luxury liner, then at least a station wagon.

SPACE MAKERS

A while back I spent hours walking through rows and rows of small kitchen appliances. I was delighted to see the panoply. Manufacturers are giving us the convenience we so desperately need but not, as in times past, at the expense of countertop space. Many appliances are available that install right on the overhead hanging cupboards, so you don't have to play checkers with your

Rubbermaid instant drawers can be attached under cupboards for extra gadget and utensil storage.

equipment come supper time. Some examples of these are toasters, mixers, can openers, coffee makers and clocks.

But, beware. In your glee to get things organized you can overdo it. There are so many machines and gadgets available nowadays, you can stock yourself right out of your kitchen: bagel makers, bread machines, pasta machines, immersion blenders, vegetable steamers, electric slicers and grinders, electric butter melter-dispensers. Unless you're making *a lot* of pasta (or whatever) on a regular basis and unless you have room to store all the equipment, you would probably be wise not to have all this stuff. In any event, before you bring a new appliance home from the store, be sure you know exactly where you're going to put it.

Here We Go Again

I know. All I do is harp, harp, harp. But the best way to gain more space is to rid yourself of C's and D's.

I have a C box in my kitchen; you can have one in each center if you need to. My C box is a large dishpan that sits on a high C-type shelf above the refrigerator. In this box is a wide variety of C items that I use from time to time: corn-on-the-cob holders,

Small appliances are well suited to small apartments. They can also provide a
mini cooking center wherever you need it.

the pouring lid from a shake-and-pour glass, extra measuring
equipment, spare can opener, skewers, donut cutter, garlic press
(now you know I'm not exactly gourmet caliber), turkey baster,
melon baller, etc. When I need something from the box I slide
it down off the shelf and select the needed tool. I use these things
so infrequently that the few seconds spent rummaging are a small
price to pay for freed-up space.

Cookie cutters and cake-decorating tools are boxed separately
in plastic containers (with lids) so I can stack them up. If you
have a large cookie-cutter collection, separate them by holiday
or season and package in separate smaller boxes and don't forget
to label them accordingly. If you have counter space, a collection
of cookie cutters looks especially decorative stored in a large
glass jar.

Another way to reduce the amount of storage space you need
is to hang things decoratively on the kitchen wall (or beams, if
you have them). This is especially effective with baskets, molds,
cookware, ladles, anything . . . as long as it's pretty and interesting. Hang it up. It's still accessible while freeing up valuable
usage/storage space for those vital A's.

I can nag until I sound like a wounded water buffalo, but the odds are against me, I know. Most of you are still going to stack up those brown paper sacks. You'll shake the crumbs from your bread bags and stuff them into a drawer. Cool Whip containers; frosting, margarine and chip dip tubs; coffee and Crisco cans are just going to seduce you and you'll quail at the thought of discarding them. (World-class junkaholics will experience the same sensations regarding cottage cheese and yogurt containers.)

What to do? Confine yourself! Designate one container or one area of space to house these addicting objects, and when that spot is filled, recycle or immediately give away the rest. When your collection begins to dwindle, start stocking up again. Just don't exceed your boundaries.

Substitute for Space

Instead of buying pans and dishes in every conceivable size, try substituting. Here are some alternatives:

An 8" × 1½" round pan holds approximately 1½ quarts. Use: 10" × 6" × 2" dish, 9" × 1½" round pan, 8" × 4" × 2" loaf pan or 9" pie plate.

An 8" × 8" × 2" square pan holds approximately 2 quarts. Use: 11" × 7" × 1½" pan, 12" × 7½" × 2" pan, 9" × 5" × 3" loaf pan or two 8" × 1½" round pans.

A 13" × 9" × 2" pan holds approximately 3 quarts. Use: 14" × 11" × 2" baking dish, two 9" × 1½" round pans or three 8" × 1½" round pans.

To determine if one pan can substitute for another, fill both with water and measure how much water each pan holds. If the volume is similar, substituting is OK. You may need to adjust baking times, depending on the size of the dish used and depth of the food. You might want to photocopy the above guide and post it inside a handy cupboard door.

If the food is deeper in the substitute pan than it would be in the size recommended in the recipe, increase the baking time. Conversely, shallower food requires shortened baking times. In any case, be sure to test for doneness according to the recipe directions.

When substituting glass for metal, reduce the baking temperature 25°. You may also need to reduce the baking time.

PHYSICALLY FIT

It seems impossible to physically fit together the odd mix of packages you need to store, i.e., boxes, bags, bottles and cans. The varying shapes force you to store unlike items behind or on top of each other. With this arrangement, one-motion storage is virtually impossible, never mind keeping things in ABC priority order.

The solution is simple: square plastic food storage containers. I have transferred all our dry food (cornmeal, tapioca, biscuit mix, oatmeal, pasta, sugar, etc.) into these durable containers. There are many brands and sizes available—and don't overlook using plastic freezer containers. These are usually found next to the canning supplies and are less expensive than Rubbermaid or Tupperware.

Tall containers are good for shelves with an expanse of vertical space between them; wide, squat containers are perfect for horizontal areas. The small round containers that have flip tops and level measuring spouts are perfect for baking soda, baking powder, cornstarch, etc. (*Note:* I like the look of uniform containers, but you might want to keep any square, original containers for easier identification.)

All the sizes combined work together to eat up every square inch of available space while allowing you to see at a glance everything the cupboard contains.

The containers can be labeled with masking tape and felt marker, labels made with a labeling gun, removable self-adhesive labels—or write on the container with permanent marker. Also, directions for making oatmeal, pancakes or cornmeal muffins, etc., are cut from the original box, slipped into a small Ziploc bag and stored right inside the container (or, tape them to the inside of the lid).

Being similar in shape, the boxes fit together like puzzle pieces. You can stack them (A's on top) or put two uniform-sized containers one behind the other, A's in front. There are other advantages: because the lids close securely, the food stays fresher and pests and excess moisture are discouraged. The food is also easier to measure.

Drawer dividers help my centers stay on track. I use standard drawer dividers in my gadget drawer so I can grab tongs, spatula or paring knife with one motion. A large plastic container (made for holding a large loaf of bread) serves as a "file" for pan lids. I slide it out, grab the needed lid and slide the container back. (Ditto with Tupperware lids.) There are also different types of lid racks you can buy. They are usually installed inside a cupboard door.

An ice cube bin sits on a shelf to corral bottles of extracts and flavorings, which can be labeled around the neckband with masking tape and marker. I have also used a permanent marker to label the tops of the bottles. That way I can slide the bin out (like a drawer), make my selection and slide the container back. The ice cube bin takes up half the amount of space a turntable would take up. Nothing gets stuck in the middle, nothing falls off the back. Another drawer divider serves as a "file" for envelopes and flavoring packets. A child's-sized shoe box also works well.

To keep drawer dividers from sliding around, use rubber matting as shelf liner. This matting is available at discount stores or office supply stores. It comes in a variety of colors and two widths, 12 inches and 20 inches. It is usually located by the contact paper or other shelf liners. Two brands are commonly found: Easy Liner and Grip Liner. (This matting keeps many things from shifting and moving: sewing machine and pressure foot, stationary power tools, bookends, booster chairs, mattresses, throw rugs, mixing bowls and cutting boards, etc. You can even put a piece under the baby in a high chair. A piece under canned goods on painted shelves will keep the cans from rusting, chipping, staining or crazing the shelf.)

If you want to keep the drawer dividers in place without spending any money, place cardboard tubes in the back of the drawer; they can be cut to fit and the dividers are easily removed for cleaning. Floral clay or carpet tape, which is tacky on both sides, can also be used and still allow the dividers to be removed for cleaning. Just be sure to use plenty of drawer dividers.

SPICY INFO

Spices pose a common storage problem. There are, of course, commercial spice racks you can purchase. Some are decorative to hang on a kitchen wall. This type usually requires that you transfer purchased spices from the original package into the decorative bottles that come with the spice rack. These organizers are

OK, but I've discovered that any jar sitting out in a kitchen gets coated with a "caterpillar fuzz" of airborne grease and dust, making frequent soap and water cleanups necessary. This problem is compounded when the spice rack is hung by the stove. For these reasons, I've chosen other spice storage options. But, don't grieve if you have to use a standard spice rack. They do have a few advantages: they're easily mounted wherever you need them and they offer one-motion storage. The cleaning problem is the only down side.

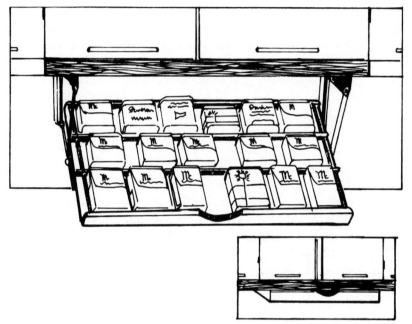

A pull-down spice caddy folds up under the cupboard and uses otherwise wasted space.

My favorite method is to keep the spices in a drawer. I use Tupperware spice containers and place the labels on top of the container so I can see at a glance the spice I need when I open the drawer. Yes, they're in alphabetical order. If you're using the original spice can or jar, you can do the same thing. Write the name of the spice using permanent marker on the top of the container.

If you frequently purchase large bottles of things like dried parsley, cinnamon, peppercorns, etc., and they're too big for the spice drawer, try this. Label the lids of the spice jars and put these oversized containers in a deep square plastic container. This box then serves as a drawer or slide-out tray which is easily used when placed on the top shelf in a base cupboard. Another option is to store the large bottles in a C location and occasionally refill the small containers that can be stored more conveniently.

Some extra-efficient cooks not only alphabetize their spices, they prioritize them. The "use all the time" spices are placed in the front of the spice drawer or on a spice rack. The less-often-used ones are placed in a more out-of-the-way place.

Spices can be organized and contained in small boxes or plastic drawer dividers fitted to size. (Velveeta boxes are just the right size.) Vinyl-coated wire spice racks are available at many discount and variety stores and are often found in mail-order catalogs. These spice caddies are mounted, using only a screwdriver, to the inside of a cupboard door. Since there are always a few inches of wasted space on the front of shelves anyway, using available (and out-of-sight) door storage is a good way to eliminate barren square inches.

A revolving square spice caddy has an advantage over turntables or lazy Susans. It holds twenty-four spice cans and the square design eliminates wasted space. Each can's label is completely visible, and because the can is contained inside the spice rack, the cans don't fall or slide off when the gadget is rotated (unlike lazy Susans).

There is also a stairstep product called Expand-A-Shelf that

A revolving spice caddy holds up to twenty-four spice cans.

puts up to seventy-five spice containers in full view (see illustration page 70). The three "stairs" expand from 14 to 27 inches to
hold cans of soup, small jars or cans of food, medicine or vitamins.
(And that's just in the kitchen!)

Many kitchens come complete with a spice storage cupboard
that's built into the front of the cupboard door. These are useful
and attractive since the spices are stored one layer deep. The
only drawback is once in a while the builder or kitchen designer
will install the specialty cupboard in an odd or out-of-the-way
location. If this is the case in your kitchen and you find yourself
setting off on a search-and-rescue mission every time you need
the fennel seed, store the A's and maybe the B's in a more accessible location and use the built-in for reserve supplies or C spice
storage. If you don't have to worry about youngsters, you can use
these customized spice cupboards for vitamins, medicine or any
other objects that will fit on the narrow shelves.

CREATIVE CABINETRY

While we're on the subject of built-in specialty cabinets, two
common ones come to mind. Many newer homes have a deep
cupboard over the refrigerator with vertical dividers. These are
designed to hold baking pans and trays. Baking pans, you'll remember, should actually be stored in the mixing center. Trays
should be stored in the serving center or close to the dishes, at
least.

These over-the-refrigerator cupboards are so useful that you
shouldn't mind the occasional dislocation, as it were. Because
they're deep, they're much more accessible than their 12-inch-
deep predecessors. Besides, whenever you're making something
that requires a baking pan, you usually need a refrigerated item
anyway. So grab the pan when you go to the refrigerator.

As for trays, is anyone in your house served breakfast in bed?
We use trays primarily when we're entertaining. So, I've decided
they're C's, and over the refrigerator is a perfect place for a C.

Another commonly seen built-in is the deep narrow drawer
designed, again, for trays and cookie sheets. These are typically
installed in a U-shaped kitchen in one of the corners instead of
those awkward and hard-to-reach dead corner shelves or turntables. My attitude toward these organizers is pretty much the
same as above. Cookie sheets and trays are B's or C's anyway.

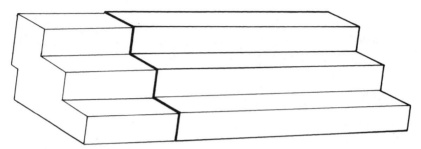

The Expand-A-Shelf expands from 14 inches to 27 inches and organizes up to seventy-five spice containers.

If your spice cupboard looks like this . . .

. . . it can look like this with an Expand-A-Shelf.

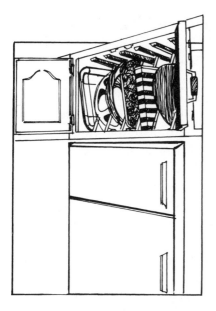

A deep divided cupboard over the refrigerator is handy for trays and baking pans.

So, if they're not located in the correct center, it's no big deal.

What I'm hoping you'll glean from all this philosophy is that frequently you have to work around existing architecture. If that is painfully inconvenient, think creatively. "What else can I put into that unit besides baking pans and trays?" For example, if the deep, narrow cookie sheet or tray drawer is by the sink, you could install a towel rack for wet dishcloths, dish towels and rubber gloves, and/or a paper towel holder. A deep bread drawer can easily be used as a file drawer for anything from receipts to recipes.

A deep bread drawer can be converted into a file drawer.

GENERIC ADVICE FOR SPECIFIC PROBLEMS

If you have a bank of deep shelves somewhere in your kitchen (making your reserve supplies difficult to see and retrieve), there are a few things you can do to make this glorious storage space more commodious. Shallow cardboard boxes can serve as slide-out trays. There are also pull-out shelves you can install. Half-shelves that I described earlier help eliminate wasted space. Store canned goods in "grocery aisles" with three inches or so between rows. That way you can store unlike items behind each other, yet you'll still be able to see and select the right ingredient. Place soup cans into a juice can dispenser (originally designed for freezer use) and they roll right out.

Another workable solution is to mark the tops of the cans (with permanent marker) indicating what it is and lay the cans on their sides, stacking as you go. The sides of the cupboard will serve as "bookends." That way, when you need a can of corn, you open the cupboard, scan the shelf and pull out the can you need.

Deep shelves, particularly those used for food storage, need to be straightened regularly. (I spend about five minutes a month on my pantry and it never gets too far out of control.) So, use some of the previously mentioned organizational ideas and straighten your deep shelves regularly, and you'll get good quality service from these storage areas.

Another common problem is the "dead corner" kitchen cupboard. If your kitchen is quite storage-worthy, use the dead corner to hold C's (preferably large ones). Smaller stored items should

Soup cans can be organized in a juice can dispenser.

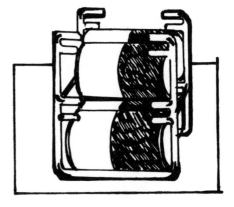

be housed in some type of container so they can be moved as one unit. If you desperately need the space, put the A's and B's in front and the C's in back.

If the corner has a built-in turntable, it will function more effectively if you straighten it periodically. Some of these turntables aren't overly sturdy, so if that's the case, you can use them for lightweight storage: cereal, plastic refrigerator containers, boxes of food, pasta, etc.

A turntable installed in a corner base cupboard eliminates dead storage space.

To keep the turntable organized, shallow boxes can be used to corral and categorize various foods—soup in one box, baking mixes in another and so on. Since the lazy Susan is round and the boxes are square you'll waste a little space this way, but if time is more valuable to you than space, the waste of the latter is OK. If you're up to a little remodeling, check chapter twelve, "Kitchen Design Ideas," for some great corner cupboard projects.

Serves You Right

It's a toss-up where you store your dishes. If you use two sets (one for breakfast, lunch and snacks, and another for dinner), it may work well to store the former close to the snack bar, cooking center or mixing center, provided you serve food to the individual plates immediately after preparation. The dinnerware, then, can be stored in a hutch or china cabinet or close to the dining room table. If you use one set of dishes (as I do) except for special occasions, I find it most helpful to store the dishes close to the sink, so they're easier to put away after a meal.

For quicker cleanup use a dishpan to cart dishes, glasses and flatware to and from the table. That way you'll be able to set and clear the table in one trip for each.

There are myriad dish organizers on the market and, I might add, many of them do indeed save space and provide one-motion storage. If you've got more vertical than horizontal space between shelves, the dividers that allow the plates and bowls to stand on edge (like file folders) work extremely well. I couldn't keep house without mine! If your space is more horizontal, there are units that function like stacking in/out baskets. Any combination of the two types enables you to squeeze out every square inch of potential space! When purchasing dish organizers it's best to buy several small units of different types rather than buy one large piece. The smaller dividers give you much more versatility.

Organizers with built-in cup hooks are not as versatile, are awkward to use and increase cup breakage. So, look out for them. Secondhand stores are full of these organizers, which leads me to believe my theory is right!

THAT'S A SWITCH!
For a refreshing change I'm going to tell you how you can *get* things instead of how to get rid of them! If you're down to three goblets, two cups (I bet you still have eight saucers) and five dinner plates (two of them chipped), here's a ray of hope. Check with your local department store, bridal registry or china shop and see if your pattern has been discontinued. If not, order the pieces you need and get your set back in honeymoon condition.

If you find, however, that your pattern is an endangered species you will probably be money ahead by selling or donating your leftovers. Then, start from scratch with a new design. If your discontinued set is missing only a few pieces, though, here is a list of companies that specialize in odd pieces from discontinued china and crystal patterns.

They recommend you send a self-addressed stamped envelope with as much information as you can scrape (that's plate talk) together (pattern name, number, color, etc.). If that information has been scoured off the bottom of the china or crystal, take a close-up photo and send that.

Locators, Inc.
2217 Hondale Lane
Little Rock, AK 72202-2018
(800) 367-9690
Fax: (501) 663-7787
They handle mainly discontinued patterns in china and crystal. They have active and obsolete sterling silver flatware patterns as well as popular active patterns in china and crystal.

Crystal Corner
P.O. Box 256
Boaz, AL 35957
(205) 593-6169
Send pattern name, number and color, or take a photo. They match china, crystal and stainless.

Popkorn Antiques
4 Mine Street
Flemington, NJ 08822
(908) 782-9631
They handle many different types of china and crystal.

Roundhill's Patterns Unlimited
P.O. Box 15238
Seattle, WA 98115-0238
(206) 523-9710
Fax: (206) 524-1252
They buy, sell and appraise porcelain, bone and earthenware. They specialize in dinnerware made by the leading potteries of the United States, England and France. Member of the International Association of Dinnerware Matchers.

SOS FOR THE SERVING CENTER
Wherever you choose to store the dishes, it's smart to keep the serving center (if you have one) close by. On the serving center list you'll notice foods usually served the way they are, directly to the plate: potato chips, cookies, prepared cereals, crackers, etc. You know, all the fattening, insalubrious, carcinogenic stuff.

Notorious in this category are potato chip bags (which always seem to rip open down the middle of the bag); cellophane cookie bags (ditto); and the bane of parenthood—cereal boxes.

When I open the Cheerios, I unfold the waxed lining with the precision of a neurosurgeon. But not the kids. It's rip open the box, tear out the lining and go for the pack of supersonic glow-in-the-dark bubblegum lying in what's left of the box. Have you ever tried to pour cereal from a box that's just been declared officially decimated? What results is four or five Lucky Charms in the bowl and three or four hundred on the table, floor and in the lap of the pourer.

Needless to say, the serving center needs help. First I enforced this hard-and-fast rule: open cereal boxes perfectly. (That's about the only rule that stands with any degree of consistency around our house.) When we buy the low-budget cereal that comes in a plastic bag, I transfer it into an empty cereal box (or plastic container) and label it accordingly. Rubbermaid and Tupperware make squarish pouring containers that are handy for storing cereal. Bags of food—cereal, marshmallows, chips, etc.—can also be hung up by using a spring-action paper clamp. Clip the bag shut and hang it up on any vertical surface.

Label each container so everyone can plainly see what's inside. If you have base cupboards with pull-out shelves, that's the best place to keep serving center food stored in this manner. Just label the lids so you'll have a bird's-eye view. Rubbermaid makes a pull-out tray that's installed, using only a screwdriver, onto stationary shelves, should you want to convert your space.

Also, Rubbermaid and Tupperware have see-through square storage containers, eliminating the need for labeling. They are, however, more expensive than brands like Action, SuperSeal and Freezette. Be sure to read the labels when you're selecting a container. Some will peel when exposed to hot foods and they may not be dishwasher safe.

BABY, IT'S COLD INSIDE

Take a peek inside your refrigerator. Those ABCs should be self-evident. Here's what I mean:

Everything in the refrigerator should have a well-defined, well-confined place. For example, the first shelf in our refrigerator is for dairy products and beverages. (The dairy products are A's and the top shelf is an A.)

The second shelf is used for leftover storage and things that need to be used up quickly like ground meat, lunch meat, etc.

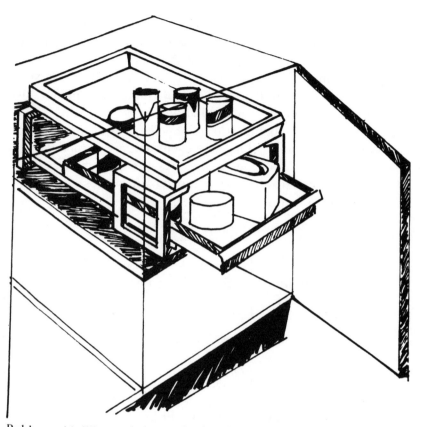

Rubbermaid slide-out shelves make deep base cupboards more accessible.

If you make sandwiches often, you might want to keep all the lunch meat, sliced cheese and condiments in one container that you can slide out and tote to the counter. The third shelf holds a large square plastic container (without the lid). The container holds all the B and C bottles and jars: molasses, soy sauce, reserve bottle of catsup, buttermilk powder, lemon juice, etc. This container functions like a drawer. We slide it out, make the selection, and slide it back in. The A bottles, jars and dispensers are stored handily with one-motion storage on the shallow door shelves. This system keeps everything contained and the contents of the refrigerator are always fairly neat and organized.

The most space- and time-saving thing you can do with your refrigerator is to be sure the door opens the right way. It should open toward the adjacent counter, not away from it. Most refrigerators sold today are two-way doors, making it easy to install the handle and door hinges on either side of the door. If your door opens the wrong way, it adds a good six or seven feet of walking distance every time you open it. So, if your refrigerator door is guilty, see if it's a changeable model and take care of that problem immediately.

The deep freeze should also be organized using freezer baskets or cardboard boxes. That way each category of food will be fenced into its own location. Sometimes a map of the freezer is necessary to speed up the search-and-seizure process.

Here's what a map might look like:

View from top: upper level

Basic Ground Beef	Roasts, Steaks	Main Dishes	
Chicken	Bread, Baked Goods	Veg.	Fruits

View from top: lower level

Pork & Ham	Bacon & Sausage	Ice Cream & Ice
Lamb	Wild Game	Novelties

You can go one step further with freezer efficiency by keeping a perpetual freezer inventory on a sheet of graph paper inside a kitchen cupboard door (or close to the freezer). On the left side of the sheet list, in alphabetical order, all the things you usually have in your freezer. The vertical columns on the graph paper are numbered along the top and bottom. Then, beside each listed item, check off the amount of that item on hand. As you remove

Pork & Ham	Roasts

Steak	Bacon & Sausage	Ice Cream & Novelties

Ground Beef	Vegetables

Fruits	Main Dishes

View of inside of upright freezer

something from the freezer, make an X through the check mark, starting at the right side of the graph paper and working to the left as things are used. Then you'll be able to see how many packages of each category are left. Also, it's only important to inventory A and B frozen goods.

This same type of inventory chart is good for anything you store. Use it for keeping a record of your home-preserved food. It will also give you a better idea of how much food to preserve next year.

You can increase the life of your chart by writing the food list in pen and making the checks and X's in pencil. This way, when food is replaced, you can erase the previous markings and indicate the amount currently on hand.

Would it be helpful to keep this inventory sheet with you? Some people keep theirs inside their planners or just grab the chart and take it to the store. That way if you see an unadvertised special on pot roast, let's say, you can flip to the inventory sheet and instantly know how many, if any, pot roasts you already have on hand. (If you keep the inventory sheet in a planner, store a spiral notebook or some Post-it notes and pencil by the freezer.) Tell family members to write down anything they remove from the freezer. Then, before you do your shopping for the week, tear off the list and update your inventory.

			1	2	3	4	5	6	7	8			
Bacon			✓	✓	✓	✗							
Basic G.B.			✓	✓	✓	✓	✓	✓	✓	✗			
Bread			✓	✓	✗								
Celery			✓	✓	✓	✓	✗						
Chicken			✓	✓	✓	✗							
Corn			✓	✗	✗								
Cube Steak		✓	✗										

Another method is to make up your week's menus, pull everything from the freezer that you'll need for the week, and store these foods in the kitchen refrigerator freezer. Mark the inventory at this time. That way the food will be handy come mealtime and you won't have to worry about whether someone remembered to mark off the chicken they pulled from the freezer.

HINTS FOR A HASSLE-FREE KITCHEN

- An ice cube bin holds approximately three dozen eggs and can be a great step-saver if your cooking center and your refrigerator are yards apart. Just cart the ice cube bin to the desired center. This is a lot easier than trying to juggle a handful of eggs.
- If you make sandwiches very often, keep a square plastic container filled with all the necessary condiments. It's easier to grab a tray than individual bottles.
- Buy jelly in a squirt-type dispenser or transfer it into a clean (labeled) catsup dispenser. Squirting the jelly eliminates the use of a knife so there are no more toast crumbs or pieces of butter or peanut butter floating around in the jelly.
- A shower cap is a great bowl cover, or can be used to cover cut watermelon or a stack of paper plates on the picnic table. You can use one to cover the bowl you're whipping cream

in. Punch the beaters through the shower cap, put the cap over the bowl and beat away with no splatters.

- A rubber band placed kitty-corner over the corners of the cutting board will keep it from slipping.
- A dampened sponge makes a good spoon rest, and you can wipe up spills as you go.
- Snap a plastic lid over the bottom of your flour sifter. This keeps your counter clean when you set it down. (I keep my sifter right inside the flour container.)
- Store a set of measuring spoons right by the spices. Toss a set into the spice drawer or hang them in the spice cabinet.
- No space to store onions, potatoes, fruits, etc.? Hang attractive woven straw or jute bags or baskets on pegs. (A colorful Shaker peg rack is especially decorative.) These will also hold tea towels, rolled placemats and napkins. You can grab the whole tote when you're ready to work.
- Make new red markings on your plastic measuring cups by painting nail polish over the raised marking. When dry, scrape the polish off the raised markings and the background will illuminate the measurement, making it easier to read.
- Use an old drip coffeepot to hold fat for deep frying. Pour the used fat into the pot—the strainer strains it. Clean out the strainer and store the coffeepot in the refrigerator. When deep frying again, heat the solidified fat right in the coffeepot and pour into your electric frying pan or deep saucepan. This eliminates the need for a space-eating deep fryer.
- This isn't necessarily a kitchen tip, but it's a good one. Coffee filters are perfect for covering drainage holes in plant pots. Put the filter in the pot before you add the potting soil. The filter allows the water to drain from the plant while it keeps the soil inside.
- Margarine containers are just the right size for individual servings of ice cream, pudding, Jell-O, leftovers or what-have-you. That way you eliminate the mess people make when they want to dish up something. Be sure to label accordingly.
- Store cookies (three or four per serving) in sandwich baggies. It's a lot less messy than having the kids drag the whole

bag of cookies around. Also, you have more control over how many cookies they eat.

- Color code your food. Tie the beef with a red cord, pork with blue and so on.
- Self-adhesive squares of cork or carpet make great bulletin boards for shopping lists, coupons, messages, freezer inventory, calendar, job charts, etc. If you want, keep them out of sight inside a cupboard door.
- Hang helpful charts inside your cupboard doors: equivalent measures, substitutions, calorie counter, freezing and roasting directions, metric conversion table and often-used recipes.
- To keep your plastic or paper bag problem under control, donate your grocery bags to a charitable organization. They are always in need of bags for their customers. Also, canvas shopping bags that you reuse will keep you from accumulating so many of the plastic or paper variety.
- Heavy plastic floor runners make good shelf lining for pots, pans and canned goods. Other options are self-adhesive floor tiles or carpet squares, oilcloth, vinyl, vinyl wallpaper, etc. When laying the self-adhesive type of shelf liner, cut off only a one-inch border instead of peeling off the entire piece of backing. With only the periphery to adhere, the paper is much easier to work with. Another easy way to work with self-adhesive shelf liner is to measure the shelf or drawer you want to line, cut out a piece of lightweight cardboard (or several sheets of newspaper) and cover the cardboard with the self-adhesive liner. Place the covered cardboard in the drawer or on the shelf. You can easily remove it to clean under it and if you ever want to freshen or change the liner, simply adhere a new piece of the liner on top of the old one. It turns out perfect every time.
- To keep nesting nonstick pans from scarring each other, separate them with paper toweling, a paper plate or coffee filters.
- Keep a can or other container for small unidentified objects you come across in your kitchen (screws, buttons, change, game pieces, etc.). This catchall works fine as long as you periodically discard the long-standing deadwood. Also, no fair expanding this idea to two cans or three cans, or four cans, or . . .

- A pocketed shoe bag can be used to hold awkward gadgets, attachments for the food processor or vacuum, big spoons, ladles, tools, mail, receipts, bank statements, etc.
- To keep tablecloths creaseless, place an empty paper towel tube at the inside fold. Store in a drawer or hang tube and cloth over a hanger.
- To store plastic bags, try one of these ideas. Stuff them inside a paper towel tube, canister, empty Crisco can (chances are if you're saving bags, you're also saving cans) or an empty Boutique tissue box. Cut a large hole (as big as your fist) at the top of a gallon milk jug. Stuff the bags inside. Using a piece of scrap fabric about 21″ × 30″, sew a tube. Fold down the top and bottom cut edges and hem to make a casing. Run elastic through each casing and tack on a loop for hanging. Stuff the bags into the top hole and pull them out through the bottom.
- Store small plastic tubs in a dishpan. Set the dishpan on a shelf and use it as a drawer.
- Sock sorters (plastic discs with an X slit in the middle) can be used as reusable plastic bag closures. Or, cut your own from small plastic lids.
- Keep skewers in a plastic toothbrush container.
- An eyeglass case (open-ended) or leather comb case provides safe storage for meat and candy thermometers.
- Store used steel wool pads in an unglazed clay pot. The ultra-absorbent clay keeps the pad from rusting.
- When loading the dishwasher, fill it with all the small things first. If there's room for the big things, that's fine; if not, it's easier to hand wash a few large items than several small ones.
- Here are a few ideas to help you determine if the dishes in the dishwasher are clean or dirty. When you load the dishwasher put the dishwashing detergent into the detergent dispenser and close the dispenser door. The next time anyone puts dishes into the dishwasher they can look at the dispenser. If it's closed, the dishes are still dirty; if it's open, the dishes have been washed. Another method is to place a glass or cup right side up on the top shelf of the dishwasher. If it's full of water, the dishes are clean. If not, the dishes haven't been washed yet.
- Put a pot scrubber or piece of plastic canvas in one section

of the silverware basket in your dishwasher. This will keep the point of the paring knife, skewers, potato peeler, etc., from falling through.

- To keep lightweight items (like baby bottle nipples) from flying around in the dishwasher, place them in a mesh bag of the type used in the laundry.

Now that everything is humming along, all you have to do (especially until the family understands the program) is to maintain your centers with the fervor of an evangelist. Whenever you notice something out of place, quietly and quickly return it to its designated home. This only takes a second or two—a far cry from what you've just been through.

Maintaining order is like keeping your money in the bank—the dividends just keep piling up; only this interest is paid with time.

Chapter Six

Food, Menus, Meals

Q uick. For twenty points and Aunt Jemima's home phone number, give me one good reason why you should take the time to plan menus. If you're like most people I encounter, you frequently say things like, "Gee, I know I should plan menus, but I just don't have time." The reason you don't have time is because you haven't discovered just how much time planning menus can save you in the first place.

Since most of your kitchen work has to do with food, menu planning is the single most important factor in streamlining your kitchen productivity. Here are seven good reasons why:

1. Good nutrition saves time. Think about it. When you take five minutes a week (at least) to thoughtfully plan dinner menus, you're more conscious of what you and your family are eating. Meals thrown together at the last minute usually fulfill just one requirement—satisfying hunger. You know that good nutrition helps you resist sickness, increases energy and stamina, and helps reduce stress. All of these things are tremendous time bandits, so, it only makes sense to eat right in the first place and avoid the pitfalls of unhealthy eating habits. Menu planning can be the first step in a sound nutritional program.

Menu planning also makes dieting easier. With a list of organized, low-fat meals that's matched with the required ingredients, you'll be more likely to stick to your diet. Staying on top of your food preparations will motivate you to stay true to your diet instead of grabbing handfuls of chips, cookies and candy. After all, you're going to eat whatever is lying around the house. So, plan for healthful meals and stock up on their nutritious ingredients.

When you plan menus you're more conscious of minimum daily food requirements. You have enough to eat so you're not suffering from constant hunger. You also get variety—so your desire for different tastes and textures is satisfied. A haphazard eat-on-the-run plan will center your eating habits on food fancies instead of food facts.

2. Menu planning helps you reduce the number of trips you make to the grocery store and/or your neighbor's house. How many times, when you're throwing dinner together at the eleventh hour, have you discovered (halfway into the meal preparations) that you don't have a certain ingredient called for in the recipe you're whipping up? Too late to turn back, you run down to the store or over to the neighbor's to pick up the stray item. Don't kid yourself. These little detours are very costly in terms of time and often in terms of money, too.

When meals are planned in advance and a shopping list made out accordingly, there are no surprises come mealtime, especially if you mark all necessary ingredients with a red signal dot so family members won't mistakenly gobble something up before its debut.

3. Menu planning saves money. Knowing your food requirements in advance helps you cash in on coupons, advertised sales and savings due to in-season produce. Planning allows incorporation of leftovers so waste is eliminated. With your menus planned and ingredients handy, you spend less money on fast foods and restaurant meals.

4. Menu plans make the most out of what time you do have available. Check over your week's schedule and discover what time commitments are coming up. On those nights when time is short you can plan nutritious, quick meals or simple meals the kids can put together.

I've discovered on the days I don't plan anything in particular, family members fend for themselves instead of getting something ready for the entire family. Then we have several concurrent messes—none of which anyone feels responsible for—and before long the kitchen is totally out of control. A few minutes of menu planning eliminates this time-costly scene.

5. With written menu plans you're more likely to delegate some of your meal preparation responsibilities. Post the dinner menu and indicate which jobs are delegated to whom. This is

especially helpful if you're not home when the kids come home from school. Someone can scrub the potatoes, put the meatloaf in the oven and toss a salad, let's say. But if your meal plans are in your head, 100 percent of the work will be in *your* hands.

6. Menu planning makes dovetailing possible. What's dovetailing? It's doubling up your efforts, getting two for the price of one. It's starting dinner after breakfast so you'll have one cleanup instead of two. It's making three meat loaves instead of one. You're dovetailing when you make extra rice for tonight's stir-fry beef to use for tomorrow's rice pudding. (I'll give specific how-to's later in the chapter.)

7. Menu planning relieves stress. Procrastination is at the heart of a stressful life. We rush off to work or get busy around the house and put off the decision about what to fix for dinner. But as the day wears on, the harping in the mind's periphery becomes louder and louder. "What should I fix for dinner?" (If you're a mom, everyone else in the family is thinking, "What is *she* going to fix for dinner?")

Then when stomachs start to growl and hungry tempers flare, we're either seen standing by the stove scraping off the thawed outside portion of the hamburger or waiting in a long line of cars hoping that soon we'll hear those cheerful words, "Welcome to McDonald's. May I take your order, please?" Menu planning enables you to decide once what to fix for dinner and eliminates facing the anxiety every day.

TRY IT, YOU'LL LIKE IT

Perhaps I've given you a little nudge in the right direction with all this sound, logical advice. But the real conversion will come after the trial of your faith, so to speak. Give menu planning a try.

Have you ever noticed this sales pitch: "Examine this product free for ten days. If you're not completely satisfied, just send it back and you'll be under no obligation." Well, try that with menu planning. Give it a shot for ten days and see what a difference it makes! You will feel so unburdened, almost light-hearted. Let me put it this way. Remember the last time your Jell-O mold came out in one piece? Did you ever make a layer cake that didn't stick to the pan? And, how did you feel the last time you went to unload the dishwasher and it was empty? Menu planning will make you feel like that every day!

If you haven't planned menus for a while, it may seem like a slow, methodical process at first, but stick with it and see if it's not everything I promised. Every time you do it you'll get faster and more efficient. Keep reading for how-to's.

THE CHOICE IS YOURS

The next time you're watching TV, riding as a passenger in the car or taking a break at work, glance through one of your cookbooks. Using a colorful felt tip pen, draw a circle around any recipes that seem tasty and will fit your time and money budgets. Circle recipes that take less than ten minutes to prepare, not counting actual cooking time. Recipes with approximately five ingredients or less are usually the quickest and least time-consuming.

When scanning the list of ingredients notice if any are unusual or not easily available. You'll have better luck picking recipes that call for ingredients you normally have on hand. Also, does the dish require special tools, pans or other equipment? If the meal will in any way complicate your life, forget it.

Go through a few of your favorite cookbooks and recipe files in this manner. And if you spot a recipe in a newspaper or magazine, don't rip it out until you've analyzed it in light of the criteria above. As much as possible, be sure it's a winner before it's selected. When it comes time to actually plan your meals, you'll have a nice potpourri at your fingertips. Time pressure is often used as an excuse to avoid meal plans. This exercise will show you what a veritable gold mine of quick and easy recipes you have at your command.

As soon as you have a cache of recipes (both new ideas and old favorites), sit down once every week or two (or once a month) and come up with as many plans as you need. That way you can coordinate your recipes with coupons, sales and in-season harvests. Plan ten to fifteen meals and have all the necessary ingredients on hand. Then when you discover exactly what the day is going to be like, you can pick out an appropriate menu that takes into account your mood (a prime consideration), energy level and schedule.

For years, when our children were younger, I used a two-month schedule. I got two monthly calendars, the type with large squares, and wrote down in each square the meal I would fix for dinner every night for the next two months. Of course, I left a few days each month blank so I could try a few recipes now and then or use up leftovers. I was careful to repeat the family favorites every two weeks or so. Because of schedule conflicts, mood swings, sickness or other unpredictable events, it was occasionally necessary to switch Monday's planned meal with Tuesday's and so forth. But basically I made up the schedule and never planned menus again for a whole year.

If you like the rotation idea you might want to try what my sister did. She set up seasonal menu plans, one for fall/winter and another for spring/summer.

Breakfast, Lunch and Dinner

I don't formally plan menus for breakfast or lunch, but I do refer to a chart I found in my old home economic notes. Using this in unison with your knowledge of the basic four food groups will assure you and your family of a nutritious, well-planned diet.

MEAL PLANNER

	Light	Medium	Hearty
BREAKFAST	Fruit or juice	Fruit or juice	Fruit or juice
	Cereal	Main dish	Cereal
	Bread	Bread	Main dish
	Beverage	Beverage	Bread or breakfast sandwich
			Beverage
LUNCH	Soup	Soup	Salad
	Sandwich	Salad	Soup
	Beverage	Bread or sandwich	Bread or sandwich
		Beverage	Main dish
			Beverage
			Dessert, optional
DINNER	Main dish	Salad	Appetizer
	Vegetables	Main dish	Salad

DINNER	Bread	Vegetables	Main dish
cont.	Beverage	Bread	Vegetables
	Dessert,	Beverage	Bread
	optional	Dessert,	Beverage
		optional	Dessert,
			optional

For breakfast and lunch I simply refer to this chart and come up with spur-of-the-moment choices, though I'm careful to have plenty of breakfast and lunch staples on hand. Dinner plans are, however, physically written down and planned for, since dinner preparation time and cleanup is more extensive. The amount of time you spend planning is in direct proportion to the amount of time you save.

Time permitting, I prepare as much of dinner during breakfast as I can and have one cleanup instead of two. Sometimes I tape instructions to the front of a cupboard door so the kids will know what to do when they get home.

TIME-SAVING CAPERS

In carpentry, when you join boards by interlocking wedge-shaped tenons and spaces, you are "dovetailing" or making a dovetailed joint. If you interlock your knuckles, you'll get the picture of what this joint looks like. We're going to do the same thing with menu planning by meshing today's meal preparation with tomorrow's.

Now that your recipes for the week's dinners are planned, look at the list and notice any similarities. Here are some examples. How many meals require chopped onions, celery, peppers, etc.? Chop enough for the whole week and store the unused portion in an airtight container in the refrigerator or freezer. Are you planning meatloaf? It takes about six minutes to throw one to-gether (including cleanup); it takes seven minutes to make three. With only a one-minute time investment you have two extra meals ready for the freezer. How many dishes during the month call for browned ground beef? Brown enough at one time to sat-isfy your month's needs and freeze in recipe-sized portions. This practice alone will save literally hours of time.

After shopping, begin preparing food for the coming week. Check the menus, shape hamburgers, cut up steak for stir-fry, wash vegetables, bake the chicken to be used for chicken salad, etc. This is a good time to get the kids involved.

Some people enjoy the convenience of having lunch-box sandwiches ready during the week; after shopping is a perfect time to assemble sandwiches for the freezer. When packing lunches, just put the frozen sandwiches into the lunch box. When it's time to eat, the sandwiches are ready. But don't freeze mayonnaise or tomatoes, as the bread will become soggy.

Squeeze as much advance preparation from your shopping time as you can manage. My friend Sherrill comes home after shopping and cooks all the meals for a whole week. Then, after work, she pulls out one of the meals and heats it up.

Don't just think of dovetailing in terms of food; processes can be dovetailed as well. For example: What needs to be shredded, diced or chopped this week? When you're shredding cheese for tonight's tacos you might as well shred the cabbage for tomorrow's cole slaw and carrots for vegetable meatballs. As long as you have the food processor whirring, make the most of it and you'll only have to clean it once. When those future meals come up, you'll be glad you did.

What else can be done ahead of time? If Jell-O salad is planned for Tuesday night, note it on Monday's schedule in your calendar. Get it ready while cleaning up Monday's dinner. Also, after dinner is a good time to section grapefruit for breakfast or make orange juice. After any meal is a good time to make tomorrow's dessert, assemble sack lunches, make salad dressing and so on.

Baking is another process that's easy to dovetail. Let's say you've prepared lasagna. Put it (or better yet, two) in the oven and prepare oven-steamed rice at the same time. A simple reheating will have the rice table-ready for tomorrow's supper. Speaking of lasagna, I can make my quick recipe in fifteen minutes. To double the recipe (giving me a backup meal for the freezer) takes seventeen minutes.

It just doesn't make sense to use maximum preparation times for every meal you prepare when you can dovetail and make two main dishes in almost half the time. Now you can see how much time is saved by planning.

Here are some ways I dovetail our family meals. A large batch of meatloaf gives me the makings for: salisbury steaks, filled meat roll, grape jelly meatballs, manicotti, meatball stroganoff or many other main dishes. With extra mashed potatoes I can make potato puffs, hearty hamburger bake and potato pancakes. Cooked potatoes are a necessary ingredient in potato salad, scrambled eggs and potatoes, hash browns, scalloped potatoes and many more potato casseroles. Likewise, rice is simple to make in bulk. It keeps well and reheats easily. Extra cooked meat is especially good when served in a Chinese dish, stew or soup.

Get into the habit of looking at the whole week's plan as you check tonight's scheduled fare. Continually ask questions like: Will I need potatoes (or whatever) again this week? Do I need to chop, shred or dice something else? Can I use my blender or food processor for something else before I clean it and put it away?

One of the greatest aids to effective dovetailing is a plastic bag sealer. Leftover (or planned-over) food is placed in a "boiling bag" and then it's sealed with the aid of a bag sealer. The food can be refrigerated or frozen. When it's time to reheat this food, just drop the bag into a pan of boiling water. The added advantage is there's no cleanup.

Bag sealers are widely available (usually under twenty dollars) at discount or variety stores everywhere. Their compact design makes them easy to store, or they can be mounted on a wall near an electrical outlet.

If you really take off with the dovetailing idea (and you should), you might find it helpful to keep an additional form that lists the prepared dishes in your freezer. This list will serve as a reminder of stored foods and may well come to your rescue when you're in a pinch and need a good meal fast. (To determine the shelf life of frozen foods, consult your cookbook.) I've included a sample form in this chapter.

MANAGING YOUR RECIPE COLLECTION

Recipes can certainly add to a kitchen clutter problem. Most of us rip out one delicious-sounding recipe after another, thinking this is the one that will hurtle us to fame and get us a spot on "Good Morning, America."

We hoard those helpful little booklets endemic to every woman's magazine. There's the sweetened condensed milk booklet, Jell-O pudding file cards, instructions for making those Bisquick Impossible Pies, the complete chocolate lover's guide.

The Chubby Gourmet whips up a masterpiece on TV and we feverishly scribble down a record of his every move. Luncheon dates with friends provide us with yet another source of recipes. Our friends share their latest find and we grab whatever's handy—checkbook deposit slips, napkins, shopping bags—and write down the details. We tear into food packages, ripping off the great recipes located on the back. We have stacks of once-irresistible cookbooks and file boxes crammed with our good intentions. We were going to try those recipes someday.

Where do you put all this paper? How do you keep your kitchen from looking like the dead-file storage warehouse at American Express? There are a few logical solutions, none of which suggest tossing recipes into a drawer, shoving them in between cookbook covers, or wedging them into file boxes!

PREPARED DISHES IN FREEZER

Name of Dish	Date Prepared	Number of Servings	Use by Date

If you want to save recipes and still be able to find them in anything less than three hours, you need to round up a few simple supplies. Get a stack of file folders and give them the following headings (or make up your own): appetizers and dips, beverages, biscuits and bread, breakfast, cakes and frostings, casseroles, cookies, desserts and puddings, meat, fish, poultry, pies and pastries, salads and dressings, sandwiches, sauces, soups and stews, vegetables, miscellaneous. Stand them up in a plastic vegetable bin, dishpan, cardboard box, hanging file box or expanding file. Now when you come across a new recipe you'll have a logical and efficient holding place for it.

Next, go through your recipe card file and toss out anything you don't want. Then, pull out every recipe you have never tried and file them according to the categories in the file folders.

Convert an extra drawer into a recipe card file.

Pick up a pack of preprinted recipe card dividers with headings similar to the ones you put on the file folders, and file the remaining tried and true "keepers" behind the tabbed dividers in the card file. For a large collection, use a kitchen drawer.

Now that the box is organized, use it only for the family favorites—the standards you've always relied on. Don't clutter up the card file with recipes you've never tried or will likely never use, even if they're given to you on a recipe card.

If you're a booklet saver (and who isn't), you'll need an expanding file (with one large pocket) to house your collection. The file is sturdy enough to stand on a shelf next to the cookbooks and its open-top design makes it easy to flip through your collection and choose just the booklet you're looking for.

Now, take a look at your cookbook collection and divide it into A and C stacks. The A's and B's stay in the kitchen, the C's are out. Put them with your other books in another room. They'll still be available for occasional use or perusal without wasting potentially functional usage/storage kitchen space.

From this point on, whenever you get a new recipe idea take an extra two seconds and place it in the proper file folder. When you try the recipe and like it, copy it onto an index card (or affix the recipe itself to the card) and file it in the card file of tried-and-true favorites. If the recipe was undesirable for some reason, throw it out . . . now.

Here are a few variations: Rather than keep your tried-and-trues in a card file, print the recipes on Rolodex cards and snap them into the Rolodex file. (Or get a Rolodex punch that will punch index cards to fit into a Rolodex file. That way, you won't have to recopy recipes that you've already got on recipe cards.) The Rolodex file stays open, keeping the recipe card visible. The card file always stays organized because you never have to take out and refile recipe cards.

Or, try this: Put the recipes into magnetic photo albums. One TV anchor I know has an efficient system. She keeps vegetable and salad ideas in a green book; meat and main dishes go in the red book; desserts go in the yellow one; and so on.

Another idea is to store recipes in plastic sheet protectors placed in categories in a looseleaf notebook. The recipes stay clean, the book opens flat and you can keep any pictures or detailed directions that are printed with the recipe.

Your card file can serve as a complete recipe index. If you can't remember which cookbook has your favorite recipe for beef Stroganoff, let's say, make up a card for the file:

Beef Stroganoff
Company's Coming, page 43

Here's a painless way to get your recipe collection transferred onto cards: Whenever you go to a cookbook to get a recipe, take a few minutes and write the recipe on a card. In six months, or so, your whole collection will be in one location. If you're cramped for space, you'll be able to remove all your cookbooks from the kitchen and rely only on your card file.

Use the margins in your cookbooks and recipe cards to record the following information: the time it takes to prepare the dish and uses of the dish as a leftover. It also helps to mark the ingredients located in the refrigerator with a yellow highlighter pen so you can gather them up in one trip and bring everything to the mixing center. (This idea would fall under the category of extra credit, or going the second mile.)

To encourage yourself to try new recipes, here's an idea: Whenever you get a new recipe, post it on the refrigerator and give yourself one week (or so) to try it. When the designated time is up, if you still haven't tried it, throw it out.

Now, if you're computer literate, you can ignore the several preceding paragraphs and get a software program that will do all the work for you. It'll store your recipes so you can find them quickly, help you plan menus and prepare a shopping list for you. Many of the programs come with recipes included. Be sure to get a program that allows you to add as many of your own favorites as you'd like to add.

A good way to perk up banal, boring meals is to periodically review those quick recipes you circled earlier. There's nothing like a few new ideas to rekindle your interest and motivation.

Menu Selection Sheets

Menu selection sheets are real time-savers, but because they are a little extra work they will probably only appeal to second-mile-goers. Menu selection sheets are lists of all the main dishes we eat for dinner. The dishes are listed by protein category: beef, ground beef, cheese and eggs, chicken, pork and ham, fish and seafood. I've also made listings for side dishes, particularly those featuring potatoes, rice and dried beans.

Contained on the menu selection sheets are: the name of the dish, ingredients called for, reference (tells me where the recipe is located) and whether the major portions of the dish can be used in another form as a leftover. I've included a sample form for you to photocopy. Start one sheet for each category: beef, chicken, fish, etc.

If you don't have time to fill out all the forms in one fell swoop, just add to it whenever you have a few extra minutes. One woman wrote to say how much she enjoyed using her menu selection sheets. She filled out her forms while commuting back and forth to work and said it only took her about two weeks to complete the project.

Menu selection sheets have many benefits, the obvious being a tremendous meal-planning assistance. When planning your meals, just flip through the sheets and all the choices are right there in front of you. No need to rely on memory or pore over a stack of books or index cards. If you keep the sheets handy in your planner, you can plan meals wherever you are and capitalize on odd moments—moments that would otherwise be wasted.

If you notice a sale on round steak advertised in the newspaper, flip to the menu selection sheets to see the different ways you use round steak and you're also apprised of other ingredients you'll need to make those dishes. The ingredients list is a handy guide for using coupons and leftovers, too. (Computer literate folks can do all this on a computer!)

MENU SELECTION SHEET

Name of Dish	Ingredients	Reference	Leftover

Now that you've seen the whole picture, here's the bare-bones plan—the minimum meal-planning requirements:

1. Look for and mark quick and easy recipes.
2. Plan menus for at least ten days.
3. If possible, begin dinner after breakfast (thaw meat, soak beans, put a meal in the Crockpot).
4. Dovetail preparations and processes whenever possible.

MORE HINTS FOR MEAL-MAKING EFFICIENCY

- If you're a compulsive recipe clipper, designate one small dishpan or box to hold collected recipe finds. When the container is full, don't save any more recipes until you've filed your collection. That'll keep the clutter within manageable limits.

- If a recipe calls for an unusual ingredient, mark it with a blue highlighter pen. Then, even without reading the entire recipe, you'll be reminded to buy the ingredient.
- Post a copy of the week's dinner menus. In the morning you'll be instantly reminded of what to take out of the freezer and what dovetailing preparations to begin. Also, diet-conscious folks can plan their "away from home" food accordingly. (Most fast food chains can furnish a nutrition-calorie guide on request.)
- Save weekly menus, grocery lists and dated cash register tapes. Staple them together and file for a quick reference for future meals and their approximate cost.
- If you want to prepare a time-consuming dish but don't have enough time, see if you can break down the recipe into two work sessions (premeasure ingredients and mix later, for example).
- Assemble all needed ingredients and utensils before you start meal preparations. How many times have you been rolling dough and had to reach (with floured hands) into the drawer to get the biscuit cutter?
- Clear, plastic report covers keep cookbook pages clean. Open the book and place the center crease of the report cover down the center of the book. Any splashes can be wiped off.
- To hold recipe cards, stand a fork (tines up) in a tall glass and place the card in the tines. Or use a magnet on the refrigerator or oven hood. If you use a metal recipe file, the magnet can be stored on the lid.
- Razor-sharp knives save time. Look in the yellow pages for someone near you who can get your knives back into shape. Thereafter, keep them sharp with one of the many knife sharpeners currently on the market.
- If you're only using one set of measuring cups, measure the dry ingredients first, then the wet.
- Rinse off utensils (knives, spoons, measuring equipment, etc.) when cooking or baking and use them again instead of reaching for clean duplicates.
- Frying food in a Dutch oven is less messy than using a

conventional frying pan. Because of its high sides, it keeps the grease from splattering.

- To cook several small dishes at once in the electric frying pan, mold small cups out of aluminum foil and place in the pan.
- A bundt or tube baking pan can be used for many things besides cakes. It holds stuffed peppers or potatoes, too. To cut corn off the cob, stand the corn on the tube and cut off the kernels; they fall neatly into the pan below. Bake meatloaf in a tube pan or set a gelatin salad. After unmolding, serve meatloaf sauce or whipped topping in the center hole.
- To easily remove baked potatoes from the oven, bake them in muffin tins.
- Spring food scoops (ice cream scoops) come in all sizes and are good measuring cups for shortening and peanut butter. (Dip the scoop in water to keep food from sticking.) They're also handy when making meatballs and drop cookies. To fill baking cups for muffins or cupcakes, use a scoop! When buying a scoop, sometimes the size (⅛ cup, ½ cup, etc.) is printed right on the package. If not, it's easy to determine the scoop's volume. Fill it with water and pour the water into a clear measuring cup to see how much the scoop holds. The ⅛ cup (perfect for cookies, meatballs, cupcakes and muffins) and the ⅓ cup (good for ice cream and dishing food servings) are the two common denominators for any recipe, so they're the most useful sizes.
- Before forming meatballs or Rice Krispies treats, slightly dampen your hands. (If you're using a meatballer, dampen it frequently during use.) This keeps the food from sticking to you or the instrument you're working with.
- Mix meatloaf with your potato masher. Or, put the ingredients into a zip-closing bag, seal the bag and knead it to mix.
- As a filling for stuffed green peppers, mash leftover meatloaf and moisten it with a small amount of tomato juice. Stuff peppers and bake. Top with grated cheese in the last five minutes of baking.
- Scrub vegetables well and cook without paring them.
- Use a french fryer basket when boiling potatoes, pasta or hard-boiled eggs. It's safer and easier than draining the hot water from the pan.

- When peeling boiled potatoes, rub a little shortening on your hands and the knife blade. This will keep the peelings from clinging to you.
- Instead of discarding potato water, add it (along with some powdered milk) to the mashed potatoes instead of refrigerated milk. Also, the potato water can be used when making gravy.
- Always cook enough potatoes or rice for more than one meal.
- Cook bacon and flash freeze. Heat separate pieces as needed.
- Drain bacon, sausage, fish or other fried foods on Styrofoam meat trays or in the top of an egg carton (line with paper towels).
- Styrofoam meat/bakery trays have many uses, and they're available in any butcher or bakery department for a few cents each. They're good for slicing tomatoes and onions (and they keep strong odors off the cutting board). They're good for transporting cookies, brownies or other such goodies and you won't have to worry about losing your dish. Use them for freezing snack bars and cookies and for mailing cookies and candy. Broken up in small pieces, the trays provide good drainage in flowerpots.
- Plastic lids are good saucers for drippy bottles. They can also be used as coasters.
- Combine salt and pepper into one shaker. A good combination is ¾ cup salt and ¼ cup pepper.
- For "instant" white sauce, mix 1 cup softened butter with 1 cup flour. Spread in ice cube tray (or other shallow container) and chill. Cut into eight equal-sized cubes and freeze. To make the sauce (medium thick), put one cube into 2 cups of cold milk. Heat, stirring until sauce is thickened. Add salt and pepper, if desired.
- The pointed end of a beverage can opener is good for deveining shrimp, hulling strawberries or ripping into boxes.
- A small crochet hook is a good tool for deveining shrimp.
- A dough cutter is handy for cutting sandwiches.
- Make miniature hamburger buns for children by cutting crusts off bread with a biscuit cutter.
- Instead of chopping eggs for egg salad, try grating them, or use a pastry blender to finely chop.
- Spray kitchen shears with cooking spray before cutting dates

and figs (or dip the scissors in water).

- Use your potato masher when making juice from frozen concentrates. You'll find the concentrate melts much more quickly.
- Make Jell-O fast in a one-quart measuring cup. Add 1 cup boiling water to the Jell-O and stir to dissolve. Note the liquid level and add ice to increase by 1 cup. Stir until ice is melted. Set in the refrigerator until firm or thick enough to hold fruit.
- Save leftover lemon, orange and lime rinds and freeze. The rinds grate easily when frozen.
- If bananas are too ripe and you haven't time to make banana bread or cookies, the banana pulp can be frozen and used up when you do have time.
- To make cinnamon toast, combine sugar and cinnamon (according to taste) and keep in an empty salt shaker. Or, if you prefer, mix the sugar and cinnamon and blend into soft margarine or butter. Store in the refrigerator. That way you eliminate the mess of sprinkling.
- A paper towel under the bottom piece of toast on the plate keeps it from getting soggy (or use a few coffee filters).
- Melt chocolate in boiling bags. These bags are also good for marinating meat. (Boiling bags can be purchased in large supermarkets and wherever bag sealers are sold.)
- Measure dry ingredients for cookies, cakes, etc., onto a sheet of waxed paper or paper towel. That way you can make the dessert using only one bowl. When making a cake, scrape the bowl clean and make the frosting right in the same bowl.
- Whenever you're making cake, cookies, brownies, etc., measure extra dry ingredients, label and store for a quick assembly next time.
- Keep a shaker container filled with flour in the mixing center. It's good for dusting baking pans or food that is to be floured before cooking.
- When making something that requires the addition of beaten egg whites (waffles, for example), beat the egg whites first, and then beat the batter. That way you will not need to clean the beaters first.
- To retrieve a piece of eggshell that has dropped into the food, use a large, clean piece of the shell. (This is the best

idea I've come across in years! It really works.)

- Slightly dampen the countertop with water and spread a piece of plastic wrap smoothly over the dampened area. (Or, use freezer wrap waxed side up.) Flour the plastic and roll out dough on it.
- Roll out biscuits and cut into squares. This saves you from rerolling the cut-up dough over and over.
- When making refrigerator cookies, press the dough into large frozen juice cans and chill. When ready to bake, open the bottom of the can and push the dough out for slicing, using the can's edge as a cutting guide.
- Store batches of cookie dough in margarine tubs in the freezer. Bake as needed for hot, freshly made cookies.
- Freeze broken cookies, and when you've got a supply, crush them and use in crumb cookie crust.
- An ice bucket makes a great cookie jar.
- Put a marshmallow in the bottom of an ice cream cone to keep it from leaking.
- When serving Sloppy Joes to children, scoop out some of the hamburger bun. That way the sandwich filling will be "in" the bun instead of "on" it.
- An ironing board set at the proper height is a good temporary table for children.
- Washcloths and hand towels are good napkins and place mats. A washcloth is also a good napkin for a lunch box meal.
- Use a loud dinner bell (or cow bell) to call the kids in for dinner.
- When teaching kids to cook, start by making snacks and breakfast.
- For busy families, try having alternate mealtimes or meal styles. Have dinner after school and snacks before bed. Or, if everyone is eating a hearty lunch away from home, have a typical lunch-type meal at dinnertime.

Chapter Seven

Grocery Shopping Savvy

I f your name is Jean Claude van Damme; if you can bench press a good-sized farm animal; if you're as good with numbers as Danny Sheridan, E.F. Hutton or Bill Gates' CPA, then you've got all the skills that are necessary to become a super-shopper.

It's a jungle out there. You face inexperienced cartpushers, kids pleading for treats (and sometimes for mercy), shopping carts that always bear to the left, sales to spot, fruit to pinch, toilet paper to squeeze. Finding the Ark of the Covenant was easier than trying to locate the Butter Buds, water chestnuts and kumquats in anything less than two hours.

Even so, I'm here to offer a ray of hope. If you're always standing in the slowest line, grabbing unpriced goods off the shelves, and causing major traffic jams at the checkout while the stock boy goes to verify the price, you (yes, you) can still acquire the spirit of adventure, the stamina and the fiscal prowess to survive the cartpushers' game. Here are the rules of play.

TO MARKET, TO MARKET WITH A LIST

Ralph Nader would be proud. I, too, will follow the other consumer advocates and recommend (insist) you shop from a list. Now, how many times have you heard that suggestion? Sure, you've heard it over and over, but making a list takes time and that's one thing you haven't got. So you skip the planning step, walk unprepared through the supermarket, and join the ranks of countless supermarket casualties. Seeming victims of amnesia, they walk down each aisle glancing left and right like the spectators at Wimbledon, hoping the flashy displays and snappy pictures will remind them of things they need to buy.

Approximately 60 percent of shoppers do not use a list, and thus they play into the market's hands. Without a list you spend extra time in the store piling up one impulse purchase after another almost in sync with the whirr of the cash register. The longer you spend in the market's confines, the more time and money you waste.

Every trip to the store is more time-costly than you may think. Even "just running in for a few things" involves parking the car, searching the shelves, sampling demonstrated products, standing in line, traveling to and from the store, and finding the car in the parking lot.

The decisions you make in the grocery aisle usually bear little, if any, relation to your actual grocery needs. A carefully planned list puts an end to this gross waste of time. It prevents you from forgetting an important item so you won't have to squander even more time on repeat performances. Maybe you're one of the 40 percent who regularly *does* use a list. What kind of a list is it? For years I used a list where I just jotted things down as we ran out of them, and in the order in which they appeared in a recipe. Such a partial linear list could look like this:

100-watt light bulbs
sugar
lunch meat
round steak
canned tomatoes
carrots
tomato paste
paper towels
hot dogs

While shopping from a list is good, using an organized list is even better. Using this example you can see the problems you're going to have. When you're grabbing the lunch meat, will you remember that you also need hot dogs? You'll probably scan the list again, or make a trip back to the same area because you forgot the hot dogs when you were there the first time. An organized list, with like products grouped together, allows you to select needed items without having to backtrack through the aisles, fighting traffic and temptation. If I remember correctly, it's a principle of plane geometry: the shortest distance between two points is a straight line. In the grocery store the shortest distance between the entrance and the exit is a route guided by such a carefully planned list.

An easy way to make a categorized list is to divide a sheet of paper into ten general headings: breads and cereals, canned, convenience foods, dairy, frozen, health and beauty aids, household and miscellaneous, meat, produce, staples and condiments. Or make up your own categories. (A sample of such a form is included in this chapter for you to modify or photocopy.)

Another option is to divide the paper into four main food groups and add a nonfood miscellaneous column. With a generalized list like this you can go into any store and shop like an old customer without chasing back and forth gathering up products. Also, if you have enlisted help, you can tear off sections and have everyone in charge of a separate group. If other people are helping you shop, be sure that sizes of cans and packages, quantities, preferred brands or grades, and acceptable substitutes are spelled out clearly on the list.

Where will you keep this list? Hang a spiral tablet or small clipboard on the inside of your mixing center cupboard door and attach a pen or pencil to it. (Use self-adhesive Velcro.) This will serve as a perpetual grocery list for the whole family. Tell them what it's for and ask them to jot down anything they use up or notice is in short supply. Don't forget to include things you notice as you're working around the house: toothpaste, laundry detergent, notebook paper, silver polish, plant food, etc. Then, before shopping, take this perpetual list and transfer it to the categorized form, also adding the list of ingredients needed for any upcoming planned menus. (To streamline this process and eliminate transferring the list, keep a supply of categorized forms on the clipboard and tell the family to list things right on the form in the proper category. This takes some skill and a lot of trust!) Now, you're ready to go shopping. Grab the clipboard and you're off! Aside from making you look like the patron saint of the supermarket, the clipboard is quite handy. The clip holds coupons you're planning to use, bottle deposit receipts or any loose papers regarding in-store premiums or promotions (i.e., cash register receipts, premium stamps, milk club card, etc.). It stands in the child's seat in the cart and is always in full view. A pen is attached to the clipboard with Velcro, making it easy to cross things off as

Breads and Cereals

_____

_____

_____

_____

_____

Canned Goods

_____

_____

_____

_____

Convenience Foods

_____

_____

_____

_____

Dairy Products and Eggs

_____

_____

_____

_____

Frozen Foods

_____

_____

_____

_____

_____

Health and Beauty Aids

_____

_____

_____

_____

Household and Miscellaneous

_____

_____

_____

_____

Meat

_____

_____

_____

_____

Produce

_____

_____

_____

_____

Staples and Condiments

_____

_____

_____

_____

you pull them from the shelves. (Cross things off the list rather than checking them off. Items just checked are read over and over. Don't waste time reading things already in the cart—cross the items off the list.) Using a clipboard is much better than juggling a list in your hand that inevitably will be ripped, mangled and chewed on before you even get to the gumball machines.

Some people like to write their lists on envelopes and slip coupons and notes for other errands inside. If this is your wont, just clip a stack of envelopes to the clipboard and hang it in the mixing center. When you leave the store, the envelope fits easily into your pocket or purse. With the popularity of various types of planners on the market, many people keep their lists in a section of their planning notebooks. (This, however, requires that you have a place in the kitchen where family members can note things that are needed.) Having the forms in a planner allows you to plan menus and shopping lists even when you're not home. No matter what system you decide to use, the most important thing is to always shop from an organized list. If you pursue that objective alone and ignore what I'm about to recommend, that's OK. Nevertheless, two more steps will help you maximize your shopping efficiency and minimize the amount of time you spend in the store. These suggestions require a slight time investment, so I'm afraid three-quarters of you will likely read through the following advice and consider it good material for a remake of "The Twilight Zone." Although I must admit having a penchant for this kind of stuff, I have found these methods enormously successful.

Fasten your seat belts. Here we go. You may never run out of bread again. Once upon a time I dreamed about the hours I would save if we never ran out of bread, dishwasher detergent or potatoes. Considering the prospect motivated me to action. I went to a large supermarket in our town and got a list of products sold. This list had products organized by category. I scanned the categorized list and wrote down everything our family would likely ever buy in a grocery store.

I typed up the list and put it in a section of my planning notebook. Using a highlighter pen, I highlighted the items that I considered A's—things I never wanted to run out of again (bread, milk, eggs, ground beef, laundry detergent, etc.). Here's how the system works. I always keep at least one of each of those A's in stock and one in use. For example, I never want to run out of toothpaste again, so I keep one tube in use and one, at least, in the supply cupboard. When the one in use is gone, I get the reserve tube and add "toothpaste" to the weekly shopping list. If you have ample storage space, you can have more than one backup item stored. However, to keep your stockpile supplied, add each depleted product to the shopping list as soon as it's used up.

This master list has come to the rescue many times. Occasionally I go through the list, checking it against the supplies on the shelves, just to make sure we've got at least one of the A's in reserve. Whenever you're short of funds, you'll automatically know where to spend the money you do have—on those A's. And if you're occasionally impulsive and stop off at a store unprepared, flip to your list and use it as a guide. Even this insouciant approach is better than relying on memory alone. Using a computer, I made an alphabetized version of this same master shopping list. Here's how I use that list. We usually shop at one of three supermarkets, so I went through each store and wrote down

IGA	Kroger	Joe's Market	STORE GUIDE
15	6A	6	Air Freshener
12	14B	7	Aluminum Foil
13	15A	4	Ammonia
3	2B	sw	Applesauce
9	8A	1	Aspirin
16	13H	ww	Baby Food
NWWSEN		1	Bacon

			Store Guide Form

roughly how the store was organized. (Basically, I just copied down the overhead hanging signs that tell you what's in each aisle.) Then using the alphabetized list, I transferred the information to a store guide form (see the sample form included in this chapter). Now, I know when I'm at Joe's Market, for example, the sweet pickles are in aisle 3A, the bread in 4B and the mascara in 15A. This has become a master map kept in my planning notebook. This works perfectly when directing your "help." Not only can you tell someone else what to go get, you can tell them exactly where it's located. Some products are not necessarily located in an aisle. In those cases, refer to the northwest wall (NWW), southeast entrance (SEE), etc.

With an alphabetized and categorized list and blank store guide form included in this chapter, I've really done most of the work for you. All you need to do is photocopy a few store guide forms, fill in your list of selected grocery products (using the alphabetized list as a reminder), then add the store's layout. In the illustration, by the way, I've listed the products according to how our family refers to them. Either the alphabetized or categorized master list can be pared down and customized to suit your needs, or duplicated and hung up in the mixing center to serve as your grocery list. (If your list won't fit on one page, have it reduced at a quick copy outlet.) Just check off the items you need to purchase.

If you want to save yourself the time and trouble of making up such a store guide form, check with the customer service department of your favorite grocery stores. They may have store maps (or product location lists) available. Also, these will be periodically updated if the store moves things around. Another way to use this master list is to put it into a plastic sheet protector and mark it with a grease pencil—you'll have a preprinted shopping list you can erase and use again and again. I'm not advocating that you get carried away with organizing your list; too much organizing is as wasteful as none. Careful inventory helps you get everything you need in as few trips as possible and helps you go quickly. If you can do that, no further organization is necessary.

MASTER GROCERY LIST

Air freshener	Beets
Aluminum foil	Biscuit mix
Ammonia	Bisquick
Applesauce	Bleach
Aspirin	Blueberries, canned
Baby food	Bouillon cubes
Baby formula	Bread
Bacon	Bread crumbs
Baked beans	Bread dough, frozen
Bakery (fresh)	Broccoli, frozen
Baking chocolate	Brooms
Baking powder	Brown sugar
Baking soda	Buns
Barbeque sauce	Burritos
Bar soap	Butter
Bathroom tissue	Butter Buds
Beans	Buttermilk
Beans, dried	Buttermilk, powdered
Bean sprouts	Cake decorations
Beef, dried	Cake mixes

Candy
Canned biscuits
Canned fruit
Canned vegetables
Carpet Fresh
Cereal, boxed
Charcoal and lighter fluid
Cheese
Cheese spreads
Chee-tos
Cheez Whiz
Chicken, canned
Chili
Chili beans
Chili sauce
Chinese food
Chocolate, baking
Chocolate chips
Chop suey vegetables
Chow mein noodles
Clams, canned
Clams, fresh
Cleaners
Cleanser
Cocoa
Cocoa mix
Coconut
Coffee
Cookie mixes
Cookies
Cooking spray
Cooking utensils
Cool Whip
Corn
Corn bread mix
Cornmeal
Corn starch
Corn syrup
Cosmetics
Cottage cheese

Crab, canned
Crab, fresh
Cream
Cream cheese
Creamed corn
Cream of Wheat
Croutons
Cupcake cups
Dairy products
Deodorant
Desserts, frozen
Dietetic foods
Dinners, frozen
Dips
Dishwasher detergent
Dishwashing liquid
Disposable diapers
Distilled water
Dried beef
Dried fruit
Drink mixes
Eggs
Enchilada sauce
Enfamil
English muffins
Evaporated milk
Fabric softener
Feminine hygiene products
First aid
Fish, fresh
Fish, frozen
Flour
Foil
Freezer wrap
French fries
Fried rice
Fritos
Fruit, canned
Fruit cocktail
Fruit, dried

Fruit, fresh
Fruit, frozen
Fruit rolls
Gelatin
Gourmet foods
Graham crackers
Granola bars
Gravy, canned
Gravy mixes
Green chilies
Hair care products
Hair spray
Ham
Hardware
Honey
Hot dogs
Ice cream
Ice-cream cones
Ice-cream toppings
Insecticides
Jam
Jell-O
Jelly
Juice, baby
Juices, bottled
Juices, canned
Juices, frozen
Karo syrup
Ketchup
Kidney beans
Kitty litter
Kleenex
Kool-Aid
Laundry detergent
Lemon juice
Lentils
Light bulbs
Liquid hand soap
Lotions
Lunch bags

Luncheon meat
Macaroni and cheese
Malt-O-Meal
Mandarin oranges
Maraschino cherries
Margarine
Marinade mix
Marshmallows
Matches
Mayonnaise
Meat
Meat, canned
Melon balls
Mexican food
Milk
Milk, powdered
Mixed vegetables
Mops
Mouthwash
Mushrooms
Mustard
Napkins
Noodles
Nuts
Oatmeal
Olive oil
Olives
Onion rings, canned
Onion rings, frozen
Oysters, canned
Oysters, fresh
Pancake mix
Pantyhose
Paper cups
Paper plates
Paper towels
Parmesan cheese
Pasta
Peaches, canned
Peanut butter

Peanuts
Pears, canned
Peas, canned
Peas, dried
Pepper
Pet food
Pharmacy
Picante sauce
Pickles
Pie crusts
Pie filling, canned
Pimentos
Pineapple, canned
Pizza, frozen
Pizza mix
Pizza Quick
Plastic bags
Plastic scrubber
Plasticware
Plastic wrap
Plums, canned
Popcorn
Popsicles
Pork and beans
Potato chips
Pot pies
Poultry
Powdered buttermilk
Powdered milk
Powdered sugar
Preserves
Pretzels
Prewash spray
Produce
Pudding, canned
Pudding mix
Pumpkin, canned
Q-Tips
Raisins
Raspberries, frozen

Razors
Refried beans
Relish
Rice
Rice-A-Roni
Ritz crackers
Romano cheese
Salad dressing mixes
Salad dressings
Salmon, canned
Salmon, fresh
Salsa
Salt
Saltines
Sanitary napkins
Sauce mixes
Sauerkraut
Sausage
Sausage, canned
Seafood, fresh
Seasoning mixes
Shampoo
Shaving aids
Shortening
Shrimp, canned
Shrimp, fresh
Shrimp, frozen
Soda crackers
Soft drinks
SOS
Soup, canned
Soup, dry
Sour cream
Soy sauce
Spam
Spices
Starch, laundry
Stews, canned
Straws
Stuffing mix

Sugar
Sunflower seeds
Sweet potatoes, canned
Sweet-sour sauce
Tabasco sauce
Taco sauce
Taco shells, boxed
Taco shells, fresh
Tampons
Tartar sauce
Tater Tots
Teriyaki sauce
Toilet bowl cleaner
Toilet paper
Tomatoes, canned
Tomato paste
Tomato sauce
Toothpaste
Tortilla chips
Tortillas, boxed
Tortillas, fresh
Trash can liners
Tuna

TV dinners
Vanilla
Vegetable oil
Vegetables, canned
Vegetables, fresh
Vegetables, frozen
Vinegar
Waffles, frozen
Water chestnuts
Wax paper
Wet wipes
Wheat germ
Wheat Hearts
Wheat Thins
Whipped topping, boxed
Whipping cream
Windex
Worcestershire sauce
Yams
Yeast
Yogurt
Ziploc bags

CATEGORIZED MASTER LIST

BREADS AND CEREALS

Bakery (fresh)   _____
Bread   _____
Bread crumbs   _____
Buns   _____
Cereal   _____
Cream of Wheat   _____
Croutons   _____
English muffins   _____
Malt-O-Meal   _____
Oatmeal   _____
Tortillas, fresh   _____
Wheat Hearts   _____

CANNED GOODS

Applesauce
Baby food
Baby formula
Baked beans
Beans
Bean sprouts
Beets
Blueberries, canned
Bouillon cubes
Chicken
Chili
Chili beans
Chinese food
Chow mein noodles
Clams
Corn
Crab
Creamed corn
Dried beef
Enchilada sauce
Evaporated milk
Fruit, canned
Fruit cocktail
Gourmet foods
Gravy
Green chilies
Juice
Kidney beans
Mandarin oranges
Meat
Mexican food
Mixed vegetables
Mushrooms
Onion rings
Oysters
Peaches
Pears
Peas
Pet food

Picante sauce
Pimentos
Pineapple
Plums
Pork and beans
Pumpkin
Refried beans
Salmon
Salsa
Sauerkraut
Sausage, canned
Shrimp
Soup
Spam
Stews
Sweet potatoes
Sweet-sour sauce
Taco sauce
Teriyaki sauce
Tomatoes
Tomato paste
Tuna
Vegetables
Water chestnuts
Yams

_____
_____
_____
_____
_____
_____
_____
_____
_____
_____
_____
_____

CONVENIENCE AND SNACK FOODS

Cake decorations
Cake mixes
Candy
Chee-tos
Cocoa mix
Cookie mix
Cookies
Corn bread mix
Cupcake cups
Dried fruit
Fritos
Fruit rolls
Graham crackers
Granola bars
Ice-cream cones
Ice-cream toppings
Kool-Aid
Macaroni and cheese
Marshmallows
Nuts
Peanuts
Pizza mix
Pizza Quick
Popcorn

Potato chips
Pretzels
Pudding, canned
Pudding mix
Raisins
Rice-A-Roni
Ritz crackers
Salad dressing mixes
Saltines
Sauce mixes
Seasoning mixes
Soda crackers
Soft drinks
Stuffing mix
Sunflower seeds
Tortilla chips
Tortillas, boxed
Wheat Thins
Whipped topping, boxed
_____
_____
_____
_____
_____

DAIRY AND EGGS

Biscuits, canned
Butter
Butter Buds
Buttermilk
Cheese
Cheese spreads
Cheez Whiz
Cottage cheese
Cream
Cream cheese
Dips

Eggs
Milk
Parmesan cheese
Pudding
Romano cheese
Whipping cream
Yogurt
_____
_____
_____
_____

FROZEN

Bread dough	Popsicles
Broccoli	Pot pies
Burritos	Raspberries
Cool Whip	Shrimp
Dinners	Strawberries
Fish	TV dinners
French fries	Vegetables
Fruit	Waffles
Ice cream	Whipped topping
Juice	_____
Melon balls	_____
Onion rings	_____
Pie crusts	_____
Pizza	_____

HEALTH AND BEAUTY AIDS

Aspirin	Pharmacy
Bar soap	Razors
Bathroom tissue	Sanitary napkins
Cosmetics	Shampoo
Deodorant	Shaving aids
Feminine hygiene products	Tampons
First aid	Toilet paper
Hair care products	Toothpaste
Hair spray	_____
Kleenex	_____
Liquid hand soap	_____
Lotions	_____
Mouthwash	_____
Pantyhose	_____

HOUSEHOLD AND MISCELLANEOUS

Air freshener	Brooms
Aluminum foil	Carpet Fresh
Ammonia	Charcoal and lighter fluid
Bleach	Chore Girl scrubber

Cleaners
Cleanser
Cooking utensils
Dietetic foods
Dishwasher detergent
Dishwashing liquid
Disposable diapers
Distilled water
Fabric softener
Foil
Freezer wrap
Hardware
Insecticides
Kitty litter
Laundry detergent
Light bulbs
Lunch bags
Matches
Mops
Napkins

Paper cups
Paper plates
Paper towels
Plastic bags
Plastic scrubber
Plasticware
Plastic wrap
Prewash spray
SOS
Starch
Straws
Toilet bowl cleaner
Trash can liners
Wet wipes
Windex
Ziploc bags

_____
_____
_____
_____

MEAT, FISH, POULTRY

Bacon
Beef
Chicken
Clams
Crab
Fish
Ham
Hot dogs
Luncheon meat
Salmon
Sausage
Seafood

Shrimp
Turkey

_____
_____
_____
_____
_____
_____
_____
_____
_____
_____

PRODUCE
Fresh fruits and vegetables

STAPLES AND CONDIMENTS

Baking chocolate
Baking powder
Baking soda
Barbeque sauce
Biscuit mix
Bisquick
Brown sugar
Buttermilk, powdered
Chocolate, baking
Chocolate chips
Cocoa
Coconut
Coffee
Cooking spray
Cornmeal
Corn starch
Corn syrup
Flour
Gelatin
Honey
Jam
Jelly
Karo syrup
Ketchup
Lemon juice
Maraschino cherries
Marinade
Mayonnaise
Mustard
Noodles
Olive oil

Olives
Pancake mix
Pasta
Peanut butter
Pepper
Pickles
Pimentos
Powdered buttermilk
Powdered milk
Powdered sugar
Preserves
Relish
Rice
Salad dressings
Salt
Shortening
Spices
Sugar
Tabasco sauce
Tartar sauce
Vanilla
Vegetable oil
Vinegar
Wheat germ
Worcestershire sauce
Yeast
_____
_____
_____
_____
_____

TO COUPON OR NOT TO COUPON

There has been a resurgence of interest in the cash-off coupon, few home managers can knowingly toss one out without suffering pangs of guilt, sweaty palms or muscle spasms. To silence the harping, we usually rationalize by whispering, "I just don't have time to mess with coupons." And, maybe you don't.

Effective use of coupons does, indeed, take time. The experts claim you can save an average of 30 percent on your total grocery bill just by using coupons and refund offers. To realize this savings, however, you must file and trade coupons and refund offers, save refund qualifiers (boxes, labels or virtually any other part of the product packaging), subscribe to at least one refunding newsletter, and carefully organize and execute shopping trips.

To do this right takes approximately five hours a week. That is a big time investment, but many refunders enjoy it as an exciting hobby, one that offers money in the mailbox almost every day. Still others treat couponing and refunding as an at-home, part-time job. A few coupon queens have worked so hard and profited so well they now have it as a full-time job. If you're interested in pursuing this savings plan seriously, I would recommend you read Susan Samtur's *Cashing In at the Check-Out*. It's a short paperback that spells out all the fine points of couponing and refunding and lists several refunding newsletters you can subscribe to. (To get more information about the book or Susan's refunding newsletter, write to Susan at Refundle Bundle, P.O. Box 140, Yonkers, NY 10710.)

If, like most of us, you don't want to invest five hours a week, you can still take advantage of coupons without giving up too much free time. Though the coupons do save some money, don't expect a 30 percent reduction with my system. Here are two different ways to organize coupons.

First, purchase an expanding check file (made of tagboard) and label each pocket with various categories: beverages, cereals, condiments and staples, dairy, health and beauty aids, household, laundry, meat, miscellaneous, prepared (bottled, boxed, canned), snacks, fast food. (If there aren't enough pockets, you can make more pockets for categories by using business-sized envelopes.

Keep this file (closed with the self-closing elastic band) under the front seat of the car. (*Note:* The best way to organize cereal coupons is to keep them organized by company—General Mills, Kellogg's, Quaker, Ralston, Post, etc.—because that's the way they're organized on the store shelves.) Use this expanding file to keep the coupons organized. I save only big coupons (25 cents or more) and I never rip out a coupon for something I wouldn't normally buy. Then, put the clipped coupons in a designated place: a covered basket on the kitchen counter, in a handy drawer or in an envelope inside your purse.

Whenever you leave the house, grab the coupons. If you're a passenger in the car, you can use the traveling time to file the coupons (or pull expired ones). If you're driving, one of your literate passengers can do the filing. The coupons also give me something to do if I'm stuck waiting for someone.

The beauty of this system is that I never forget the coupons because they're always in the car. I can't begin to tell you how many times we've arrived at a store or a fast-food restaurant and wished we had the coupons with us. Now we store them at the point of first use—in the car!

If you want to take advantage of occasional refund offers you come across, make an index card for each category in your coupon file and stick it in the pocket. Here's how it works. Let's say there's a one-dollar refund if you buy three packages of Goodie Cookies and send in the proofs of purchase (POPs). Pull out the snack card and write: Goodie Cookies 3 POPs $1 refund. Then, stick the card back in the pocket. The casual couponer/refunder can also file the refund form in the pocket with the coupons. Now, let's say you're making caramel crumbballs for dessert this week and you need to buy some cookies. Pull out the snack card and see if there's a refund on cookies. You'll be reminded of the Goodie Cookie offer and purchase that particular brand.

More serious money savers read grocery ads and plan their menus around store specials. They try to match up these sales with cash-off coupons and look for stores that "double coupon." Such stores give you double the face value of a coupon. A 25-cents-off coupon would be worth 50 cents off. There are seldom cash-off coupons or refunds available for store brand merchandise. So before you buy, see if you have a coupon for a name brand. With a coupon, a name brand may actually be cheaper than a house brand.

Here's another way to store and organize coupons. Use a large loose-leaf notebook with tabbed dividers labeled with the same headings used on the expanding file. Put several sheets of heavy, unruled paper behind each divider. Now, when you clip the coupons, put them onto the sheets of paper using Post-it Glue (it comes in a stick). The Post-it Glue enables you to remove the coupons when you want to redeem them. You'll have a book of coupons you carry right to the store. Just flip through the pages and pull out the coupons you want to use. This makes the coupons easy to see and to use, but it requires a greater time investment than does the expanding file.

YOUR FOOD DOLLAR

In a *Consumer Trends* report, Louis Harris and Associates observed that saving money appears to be "out" and saving time is "in." According to the publication, many shoppers are willing to spend money if it means they can save time.

If you're part of that vanishing breed of consumer who still cares about how the food dollar is spent, here are some tried-and-true value-minded ideas.

- Always shop from a list and stick to the list. Don't be suckered into buying whatever the demonstrator is cooking up. She gets paid by the hour whether you buy the product or not, so don't feel obligated. The grocer is cashing in on the idea that if people are hungry (or tempted with food) they'll buy more. So follow the oft repeated code: Don't shop when you're hungry.
- Plan your shopping to last for at least a week. The less often you shop, the less you'll spend. Some stores will take your order over the phone, computer or by fax, then deliver it to you. Staying out of the store might help you save money— even with the cost of delivery added.

BUY THE WEIGH

- Unless the kids are trained not to grovel and beg, leave them home. They'll slow you down with their TV-brainwashed minds and wreak havoc with your budget. However, if you work out a deal such as "Everyone gets to pick out one nutritious thing this week," it can work to your advantage, especially if they'll help round up needed commodities from the far reaches of the store. If the carts at the store are not equipped with seat belts, take a man-sized belt to the store with you. Stretch belts are good, too. (The belts are good to take to restaurants, too.)
- Avoid shopping during peak periods (from 5:00-6:30 P.M.) and on weekends. These early evening hours are the times when the folks who've been wondering all day what to fix

for dinner do their shopping. They are a highly disorganized lot, so steer clear of them.

- Avoid buying food any place but a grocery store. Avoid excessive trips to restaurants and fast-food chains. The food is often twice as expensive as food you prepare yourself and is usually high in fat, sodium, cholesterol and calories, and notoriously deficient in vitamins, minerals and dietary fiber.

  You also pay more for food purchased from small stores or convenience shops. You get the most for your money when you shop at a large grocery store in a middle-class neighborhood. Avoid buying certain nonfood items in a grocery store (toys, plants, hardware and so on). These are generally poorer quality and more expensive.

- Don't pay for a flashy store layout. There was one particular market in our neighborhood where we loved to shop. It was so gorgeous! It was clean and well stocked. You felt great when you walked through the automatic electronic-eye doors. They even provided play carts for little kids to push around. But the catch was the prices. The cost of anything in that store was so outrageous they might as well have held a gun to your head, and said, "This is a stick-up!" The price stickers sneered at you as if to say, "That'll be $2.79, sucker."

  Then there was another store that one of our kids feared was a dungeon (he wouldn't set foot in it until he was seven and a half years old). The building was timeworn, the aisles were narrow, there were no bright lights or colorful banners. But the produce was fresh, the checkers were fast and friendly, and it was the best value in town. Because the square footage of the store was somewhat limited, you could get in and out quickly without having to walk past motor oil, greeting cards and furnace filters on your way to the bananas.

- Try to do all your shopping in one store. Plan your menus around that store's specials and don't chase around town picking up good deals from every merchant. This is almost always a costly mistake unless you are scrupulously well-disciplined and the stores are close together. Stock up on your favorite products whenever your store is offering a special price. Shopping the same store has other advantages as well: you become familiar with the store layout and can shop faster; you get acquainted with the personnel and know which checkers are quick and dependable. It's also to your advantage to know the butcher and the produce and bakery managers, should you have unique requests or needs.

- Be aware of regular prices so you'll be able to recognize bona fide sales and price reductions.

- Whatever is done to food before you buy it (slicing, cooking, premeasuring, prepackaging, flavoring, etc.) costs you money. Unless the product proves to be a great time-saving convenience you may want to do it yourself and save. Remember, you always pay more for individual-portion boxes of cereal, bags of chips, drink mix packets and so on.

- Read usage labels and directions. Here are three things to look for: unit pricing and cost per use, double-duty products, and consumer services offered.

- If the price difference between egg sizes is less than seven cents, the larger eggs are the better buy.

- Watch for day-old specials in the bakery section of the store. Also, the meat counter will frequently sell meat half-price when it's close to its expiration date. The meat is still good quality; just be sure to prepare it shortly after purchase.

- Buy the largest quantity of anything. It's usually cheaper that way if you can use it all. Waste is always expensive.

- Any produce sold by the piece (lettuce, two heads for $1; honeydew melon, $1.99 each; pints of strawberries, etc.) should be weighed; always buy the heaviest portion.

- Don't buy a better grade of product than you need. Flaked tuna is perfect for tuna sandwiches. There's no sense paying more for the large chunk or fancy albacore variety. Grade B (usually broken pieces) of fruits and vegetables are fine when they're going to be chopped in a salad or casserole.

- Check open codes on perishable products to make sure you're getting the freshest goods possible. A few years ago we bought a batch of canned biscuits. They were such a great bargain we picked up one tube after another. While eating them, however, we noticed they had the relative density of manhole covers. I checked the dated cans and they were just that—dated! They had lived a long, though hardly useful life, well beyond the stamped expiration date.

- To monitor your spending, shop with a calculator. Knowing your running total may help stave off impulse buying.
- Watch the checker and make sure you are charged the correct amount for your groceries. Stores with scanners are a real boon to penny-wise shoppers, but every once in a while they're wrong, too.
- If you travel a distance to reach a grocery store, an insulated beach bag or Styrofoam ice chest keeps frozen foods cold until you get home. Some people always keep a plastic milk jug filled with water in their freezers, and when they go shopping on hot days, they put the frozen jug in the foam cooler.
- If you walk to the market pulling a shopping cart, keep a plastic tablecloth inside. Should it start to rain, you'll have a way to protect your purchases. A cardboard box in the bottom of the cart will keep the grocery bags dry and clean.
- A bicycle basket attached to the wall next to the back door is a handy rack for a bag of groceries while you unlock or open the door.
- Using a collapsible shopping cart is a convenient way to get the groceries from the car to the kitchen in one trip.

See—you survived the cartpushers' game after all. Just follow the rules and you'll be a cinch to win. Though the President might not dial up your "locker room" or invite you to the White House as he does with the World Series and National Spelling Bee champs, you'll be a winner just the same. The prize? Extra cash, more free time and the confidence and skill to become the Sorceress of Safeway!

Chapter Eight

Recipes—Quick and Healthy

Years ago there was a television commercial where a woman was down on her hands and knees cleaning out the oven. She pulled her head out of the oven and said, "Be a good cook," Mother said. "You'll get a man!" From my experience, being a good cook didn't necessarily get me a man, but it ensured that every day for the rest of my life I would ask myself the question,"What are we going to fix for dinner?" That ubiquitous question began the day I started keeping house, and if that weren't bad enough, now I've added the battle of the bulge and a race against the clock.

Sure, there are times when I want to provide a hearty farmhouse meal or a gourmet feast. Recipes for those types of fare are plentiful. But many times I just want an "immediate" meal—quick without sacrificing sound nutrition. Those recipes, it seems, are a little harder to come by, so I thought I'd share some good and easy ones we enjoy. Some of these recipes are quick from start to finish. Others are put together quickly, but require longer (unattended) cooking times.

Before we get started with the recipes, here are a few time-saving ideas that will pare precious seconds from any meal preparation. To save recipe preparation time try frozen chopped vegetables, dehydrated onions and garlic. Or, whenever you're chopping onion, celery, green pepper, herbs, etc., cut up extras and freeze in recipe-sized portions in airtight containers.

Also, the take-out salad bar at the supermarket is a good place to choose sliced and chopped vegetables, shredded cheese, sprouts, olives, sunflower seeds, croutons, etc. You'll pay more than if you did all the work yourself, but it's a great way to buy a little time. For heat-and-eat pasta and rice, prepare pasta and rice according to package directions. (Rinse and drain pasta well to stop the cooking process.) Put ½-cup portions in freezer bags. Seal, label, date and freeze. To reheat, put into microwave bowl and cover with waxed paper. Microwave for a few minutes until hot. Or, steam the rice over boiling water. Drop pasta in boiling water just long enough to heat through.

Did you know you can cook rice in the oven? (Check the recipes for how-to's.) When you're using the oven for something else, why not put in a pan of rice to cook at the same time? It'll be ready for use in another dish you'll be fixing later in the week.

Meatballs can also be browned in the oven. Prepare your favorite recipe and place meatballs in an ungreased, shallow pan. Bake at 350° F for 10 to 15 minutes until meatballs are browned. (Four pounds of ground meat mixture will make about 144 meatballs. Separate into recipe-sized portions and freeze for future use.)

Whenever you have a cookie or cake recipe that calls for a greased and floured pan, try this recipe for cookie and cake pan grease. With this on hand you can grease and flour a pan in one operation. With an electric mixer, thoroughly mix 2 cups of shortening with 1½ cups unsifted flour. Store in a covered container. Use within three months.

Spice up your recipes with your own seasoning mixes. You can duplicate the recipes I'm including or you can use your own. Using my favorite spaghetti recipe, for example, I make up individual Italian seasoning packets. I put six or eight juice glasses on my kitchen counter and line each glass with a small plastic sandwich bag. Then, I get out the ingredients called for in the recipe. Into each bag I put two tablespoons instant minced onion, one-fourth teaspoon dehydrated garlic, two tablespoons parsley flakes, etc. When all the mixes are finished, I close up the bags and store them in a small plastic container.

LET'S GET COOKING

Italian Chicken

2 Tbl. grated Romano or Parmesan cheese
3 Tbl. bread crumbs
1 tsp. dried parsley flakes

¼ tsp. crushed basil
1 clove garlic, crushed
¼ cup lowfat milk
4 chicken or turkey breasts (skinless, boneless)

In shallow dish combine cheese, bread crumbs and spices. Put the milk into another small dish. Dip the poultry into the milk and coat with the bread crumb mixture. Place in ungreased 9″ × 13″ baking pan. Bake at 425° F for 10 to 12 minutes or until meat is no longer pink. Serves 4.

Hawaiian Chicken

4 to 6 skinless chicken breasts
2 cups barbecue sauce
1 16-oz. can crushed pineapple with juice

Preheat oven to 400° F. Place chicken in greased or sprayed baking dish. Bake chicken breasts for 45 minutes. Meanwhile, mix barbecue sauce, pineapple and juice. Pour mixture over chicken and cook 15 minutes longer. Serves 4 to 6.

Crockpot Turkey

1 frozen boneless turkey roast, partially thawed (approximately
   3-3½ pounds)
2 stalks celery
1 small onion
1 carrot
½ cup water
¼ tsp. crushed rosemary
1 Tbl. orange marmalade

Mix water and rosemary and put into Crockpot. Add turkey . Cut vegetables into large pieces and put into pot. Cook on low for 10 to 12 hours or until internal temperature of the turkey is 180° to 185° F. Meanwhile, melt marmalade in microwave or saucepan. Remove meat from Crockpot and brush with marmalade. (Discard liquid and vegetables.)

Fish or Chicken in Foil

1 lb. fish fillets cut into four serving-sized portions (or substitute four boneless servings of chicken)
salt and pepper, to taste
2 large carrots, thinly sliced
1 zucchini squash, thinly sliced
½ cup water, divided

Preheat oven to 450° F. Place each fish portion in the center of a piece of heavy-duty aluminum foil. Season to taste. Place vegetables and 2 tablespoons of water on top of each. Fold foil over and seal securely on all sides. Place the foil meals in a large baking pan and bake for 18 minutes. Serves 4. Variations: Any thinly sliced vegetables may be substituted for the carrots and zucchini.

Crockpot Round Steak and Gravy

2 to 2½ lbs. round steak
1 envelope dry onion soup mix
¼ cup water
1 10¾-oz. can cream of mushroom soup

Cut steak into 5 or 6 serving-sized pieces, removing fat and bone. Place in Crockpot. Add remaining ingredients. Cover and cook on low setting 8 hours or until meat is tender. The gravy is good with potatoes, pasta or rice. Serves 5 or 6.

Slow-Cooking Pot Roast

3 to 4 lbs. beef roast
1 tsp. salt
½ tsp. seasoned salt
¼ tsp. pepper
¼ cup chopped onion (or substitute 1 Tbl. instant minced onion)

1 cup water
1 tsp. instant beef bouillon

Rub meat with seasoning. In Crockpot, combine onion, water and bouillon and add meat. Cover and cook on low for 8 to 10 hours or until meat is tender. If desired, potatoes, carrots, turnips, etc., may be cut up and added and cooked at the same time. Makes 6 to 8 servings. A variation is to season beef with salt and pepper. Place in Crockpot. In mixing bowl combine 1 can vegetable soup, ½ cup water (or tomato juice), ⅛ teaspoon dried basil and 1 teaspoon dried parsley. Cover and cook on low for 10 hours or until meat is tender.

Oven Swiss Steak

1 round steak, tenderized
½ cup flour
2 tsp. salt
1 quart tomatoes, cut up
1 cup chopped celery
1 cup chopped carrots
¼ cup chopped onion
1 tsp. Worcestershire sauce
Grated cheese

Cut meat into 5 to 6 serving-sized pieces removing fat and bone. Dredge meat in flour. Place in small amount of oil in skillet and brown on both sides. Remove meat from pan and put into 9″ × 13″ baking dish. Put remaining ingredients along with remaining flour into the skillet and cook, stirring over medium heat until sauce is thick and bubbly. Pour over meat. Cover and bake in 350° F oven for 2 hours. Remove from oven and sprinkle with grated cheese. Serves 5 or 6.

Bean Soup

1 lb. dried small white beans
8 cups water
1 meaty ham bone or 2 cups diced, lean ham

1 cup finely chopped celery
1 onion, finely chopped (or use ¼ cup instant onion)
2 Tbl. finely chopped parsley
1 tsp. salt
¼ tsp. pepper
1 bay leaf

Soak beans overnight (or boil gently for 2 minutes; turn off heat and let stand 1 hour). Put beans into Crockpot and add remaining ingredients. Cook on low for 12 to 14 hours or until beans are very soft. Before serving remove bay leaf and ham bone. (If using a stovetop, cook beans for 1½ to 2 hours, or until tender.)

Layered Casserole

1 large onion, chopped (or use ¼ cup instant onion)
1 lb. lean ground beef, uncooked (or substitute Basic Ground Beef, page 134)
5 medium potatoes, scrubbed and sliced (leave skins on)
1 lb. frozen or canned corn
1 can cream of mushroom soup

Preheat oven to 375° F. Spray a 9″×13″ baking pan with vegetable cooking spray. Layer crumbled meat, onion, potatoes, corn and soup. Cover with foil and bake for 1½ hours or until potatoes are tender. Serves 8.

Oven-Steamed Rice

3½ cups boiling water
2 Tbl. butter
1½ tsp. salt
Dash pepper
1½ cups raw rice

Preheat oven to 350° F. Combine all ingredients in a 1½ quart ovenproof casserole dish. Cover tightly with foil and bake for 45 minutes. Serves 6 to 8.

Barbecued Potatoes

2 large potatoes
1 Tbl. margarine, melted
1 Tbl. honey
2 tsp. chili powder
¼ tsp. garlic powder
⅛ tsp. pepper

Preheat oven to 425° F. Wash (do not peel) and thinly slice potatoes. Spray baking pan with nonstick cooking spray. Put potatoes into pan. In small mixing bowl, combine remaining ingredients, blending thoroughly. Spread mixture evenly over potatoes. Bake 15 to 20 minutes or until potatoes are tender. Serves 3 or 4.

Quick Potato Toss-Up

3 baking potatoes (about 1 pound)
¼ cup reduced-fat Italian salad dressing
1 Tbl. snipped chives
pepper

Preheat oven to 350° F. Spray small baking pan with nonstick cooking spray. Wash and slice potatoes about ½-inch thick. (Do not peel.) Pour dressing over potatoes and toss until potatoes are coated. Put into baking pan. Sprinkle chives and pepper on top. Cover with foil and bake for 50 to 60 minutes until potatoes are tender. Serves 3 or 4.

Ranch Dressing

½ tsp. onion salt
½ tsp. MSG, optional
⅛ tsp. garlic powder
¼ heaping tsp. pepper
½ tsp. salt
½ tsp. parsley flakes

This makes one seasoning packet. To make ranch dressing, combine 1 cup buttermilk and 1 cup mayonnaise or Miracle Whip. Sprinkle seasoning into mixture and stir until blended. Low-fat ranch dressing may be made by using buttermilk made from buttermilk powder and fat-free mayonnaise or Miracle Whip.

Quick Fruit Salad

1 3½-oz. package instant vanilla pudding
2 1-lb. cans fruit cocktail, drained but reserve the juice
1 cup miniature marshmallows
1 cup coconut, optional
13 bananas, sliced

Combine reserved juice with the instant pudding. Blend until smooth. Fold in remaining ingredients. Chill until thickened. Serves 6 to 8. (To make ahead, do not add bananas until just before serving time.)

Fruit Salad With Poppy Seed Dressing

1 10½-oz. can mandarin oranges, packed in water
1 8-oz. can crushed pineapple, packed in juice (or use tidbits)
1½ cup small strawberries or seedless grapes
1 medium apple
½ cup lowfat pineapple yogurt
½ tsp. poppy seeds

Drain canned fruit and reserve one tablespoon of pineapple juice. Cut strawberries in half. Cut apple into bite-sized pieces. In mixing bowl combine fruit, tossing lightly. In small mixing bowl combine yogurt, one tablespoon pineapple juice and poppy seeds. Stir until blended. Pour over fruit salad, tossing to mix. Serves 5 or 6.

Basic Ground Beef

6 lbs. lean ground beef
2 cups chopped onions (more or less to taste)

This is a quick start to any recipe calling for browned hamburger. In large pan, brown hamburger and onion. Drain. Divide into six portions and freeze. (You can also add chopped celery or green pepper.)

It's a good idea to make up seasoning packets for anything you make frequently. There are times when I enjoy making things with all fresh ingredients, but when I don't have time, it's nice to pull out a homemade seasoning packet! Here are a few of our favorites:

Mexican Seasoning Mix

1 cup instant minced onion
⅔ cup instant beef bouillon
⅓ cup chili powder
2 Tbl. ground cumin
4 tsp. *each* crushed red pepper and oregano
2 tsp. garlic powder

Mix ingredients thoroughly and store in tightly covered container. Use 3 tablespoons to every pound of meat in chili, tacos, enchiladas, etc. (If using for tacos, add about ½ cup water with the mix and continue cooking until most of water is evaporated.)

Italian Spice Mix

2 Tbl. instant minced onion
1 tsp. salt
2 Tbl. parsley flakes
¼ tsp. dried thyme leaves, crushed
¼ tsp. garlic powder

1 Tbl. brown sugar
1 bay leaf
1½ tsp. dried oregano, crushed.

Mix ingredients and store. This makes one packet of spice mix. I use this blend for anything Italian: pizza, spaghetti, lasagna, manicotti, etc.

Nothing perks up interest in cooking more than new and delicious recipes. Give some new recipes a try and stir up a little excitement!

Chapter Nine

Cleaning: It's a Dirty Job But Someone Has to Do It!

You name it, I've cleaned it. Oh, I've had the usual kitchen messes to contend with, like corn flakes welded to cereal bowls, but I've also had my share of humdingers. Like the time one of our little "chefs" decided to make homemade fudge. He burned the candy and the pan so severely that he decided to just hide the pan. That way, so he thought, I'd forget about that pan and he could safely just throw it away. Well, getting that poor pan clean was just about a three-blimp event.

Then there was the time we were moving across the country. The kids and I came out first and Dad followed a few weeks later driving the truck. In order to save a little time, he decided to leave the eggs inside the refrigerator when he moved it. You read right. Inside the refrigerator. Well, two weeks and eighteen smashed, rotten eggs later, the truck arrived and it was time for me to set up housekeeping. Am I lucky—or what? Now, twenty-some years, thousands of meals and as many messes later I figure I know just a little about cleaning kitchens. Basically, cleaning up a kitchen is a three-step process (would that it only took three steps!):

Prevent
Schedule
Do

My first consideration in saving time is to prevent the work in the first place. Here are some prevention tricks I use in my kitchen. Even trying a few of the ideas will cut a real swath in the time you normally spend in cleaning up.

KEEP DIRT OUT

Stop the dirt where it starts—at the entrances to your home. Door mats keep your house cleaner and reduce the need for shampooing, waxing, washing floors and floor coverings. According to America's only living Mr. Clean, Don Aslett (author of *Is There Life After Housework?*), "Proper matting alone can save the average household approximately 200 hours of work a year, slow down structure depreciation, and save over $100 in direct cleaning supply costs."

Avoid using carpet remnants, mats with cloth backing, link or perforated mats. They just don't do the job of removing all the dust, dirt, fine gravel and grit that hangs onto incoming shoes. Don recommends commercial nylon-tuft mats inside the door and synthetic grass or rough-textured mats outside. They should be long enough to allow four steps on each. These mats may be purchased from a janitorial supply house or by mail.

In the meantime, start training your family to leave their shoes at the door. I have a wonderfully organized friend who has been very successful with that tactic. Actually, any fact associated with home management and efficiency Sherrill can spit out as if she were a laser printer. She keeps restaurant-sized dishpans just inside the front and back doors. Before the children come into the house, they slip off their shoes, toss them into the dishpan and enter the house. She has them so well trained they are never in the house with their shoes on. Each family member's shoes are stored in large restaurant-sized dishpans on shelves in the attached garage. Sherrill's children are no different from your kids or my kids. The difference is Sherrill. She is consistent and her training is reflected in her family's willingness to cooperate. (Get this: she has single-handle faucets in her house and everyone turns them off with their elbows so the chrome stays drip-free.) Perhaps you think that's going a bit too far, but Sherill has indeed learned the time-saving value of prevention.

Another friend of ours has an engraved brass plaque on her front door that politely asks all visitors to remove their shoes. And yes, I always wear my good socks when I go over to her house. Although a good share of house dirt is tracked in with the shoes, still more soot is coming in through poorly insulated doors and windows. Seal those openings. Keep all furnace and air-conditioning filters and vents serviced regularly. Keep dirty (I mean d-i-r-t-y) clothes, boots, shoes and toys outside. Empty the vacuum bag frequently so it won't spew dust around the house when you use it.

CLEAN WHILE YOU COOK

Every time you make sandwiches, soup or a gourmet feast, always perform the three A's of meal preparation:

(1) Fill the sink with hot, soapy water.
(2) Spread a sheet of freezer wrap on the counter (or, tear open a brown paper grocery sack).
(3) Put a temporary trash container on the floor by the center where you're working.

Nothing speeds up kitchen work quite like cleaning as you go. Do your preparations on the freezer wrap (it's waxed on one side) to keep the counter clean and free of splatters. When you're finished with a utensil, toss it in the sink of soapy water. Wipe up spills as you go, so you won't have to scrub later. Having the trash container handy will encourage you to discard opened cans, wrappers and empty jars instead of just keeping them on the counter "for now" until you clean up the kitchen.

Aside from the obvious benefits, the real advantage of the three A's is that you approach your work in an organized manner. With those three visual reminders, you automatically do things more efficiently because you're *thinking* more efficiently.

DO IT NOW

Replace things immediately when you see they've been put away in the wrong spot. Stanislaus Leszczynski said, "No snowflake in an avalanche ever feels responsible." Melt the snowflake before it has a chance to become an avalanche. Here are some specific ideas.

After using the oven, wipe it out before it completely cools down. You'll save hours of work by eliminating the eventual soldered mass. Clean your range top and drip pans daily for the same reason. I used to hate cleaning the range top. But if I do it every day, I know I'll never have to spend a block of time cleaning the stove again!

Wipe off bottles, jars, canisters, etc., before you put them away;

likewise small appliances. Don't put anything away unless it's clean, in good repair and ready for its next use.

Beat the Clock

I never realized just how long a minute was until we got a microwave. Steaming a hot dog for fifty seconds sometimes seems like forever! Many times I have had to appear on noon news programs and had only a minute and a half to deliver a message about one of my books or a product. No problem. My microwave taught me that you can say and do a lot in one minute.

When I realized I could empty the dishwasher in less time than one commercial break, I didn't loathe the job quite so much. The same goes for watering the kitchen plants, washing the kitchen sink window and appliance doors. My point is this: If you think there's just too much to do and no time to do it; if you actually abominate a particular job or jobs, find out just how much time the task takes. More than likely it's a fraction of what you imagine it to be; thus, it becomes more palatable.

Another way to reduce the time you spend cleaning the kitchen is to budget it correctly. Include cleanup time with the time it takes to make something. In other words, if you want to throw a casserole together before you leave for work, give yourself enough time to get the meal preparations cleaned up, too (whenever possible).

THE KITCHEN IS CLOSED

When you're watching TV and the picture gets a little fuzzy, what happens? Sure, the little man inside the TV holds up a sign that says, "Video difficulties. Please stand by." When you go to a store that's being remodeled, what does the management tell us? "Pardon our dust. We're remodeling to serve you better." And when you travel cross-country and the highway is ripped up, the road warriors make it OK by saying, "Road construction next 97 miles. Thank you for your cooperation."

We go along with all these excuses simply because we have no other choice. So, I figured why not do the same at home? Closing the kitchen at a certain time every night (and sticking to the rule) is a great way to keep your kitchen clean. (Admittedly this is easier if you have young children and no one working the swing shift.) Ideally, this hour should be a half hour before bed, so while the kids are getting ready, you can once and for all put the finishing touches on the kitchen knowing it will stay that way until morning.

Anyone who can't abide by this system should take an oath (similar to the one taken by adopters of Cabbage Patch Kids) that they will clean up all signs of meal preparations before they go to bed. If you're feeling especially mean, you can insist they arise early in the morning to take care of anything they neglected.

That's the textbook method for closing your kitchen. Here's a more laid-back approach. Say something like this: "The kitchen is closing in thirty minutes. If you're going to eat anything, do it now." You don't necessarily have to have a regular time every night, either. Just go with your particular mood that day. After the thirty minutes (or whatever) has passed, the person in charge of the kitchen puts it to sleep for the night.

That takes care of preventive maintenance in the kitchen. You can see how, with every little effort, hours of work, worry and frustration are excised from KP duty.

Next step: schedule.

YOUR CLEANING SCHEDULE

Some time ago I was flying out of town and made a quick stop in the airport rest room before boarding the plane. I happened to notice a cleaning schedule hanging on the wall. It included three columns.

In column one, each specific job was listed. In column two was a space to record the date and time the job was completed. In column three were the initials of the person who performed the job. The whole system was so well organized that even a person with a good deal of aspic in the place of brain cells would know exactly what to do. I wondered why it was necessary to have everything spelled out. These janitors are intelligent, hard-working people; certainly they can clean up an airport bathroom and do a good job of it. Don Aslett answered my question. Don, in addition to authoring the book I mentioned, is the president of Varsity Contractors, one of the largest janitorial service companies in the world. He told me that before their jobs are contracted, everyone knows exactly what jobs will be done, how long they will take, when and how often each task will be completed. He pointed out that in an industry where profits are made and lost, scheduling—even in such detail as the airport bathroom—is necessary to get the work done faster, better and at less expense.

I'm convinced we should take the same approach at home. Certainly, we, too, want to do things better, faster and at less expense. (I'd just settle for faster!)

I was so inspired by the airport form that I drew one up and photocopied a stack for our family to use. Now, anyone who's old enough to read knows exactly what has to be done on a day-to-day basis. If one child is assigned kitchen work for a whole week, hang up the chart as is (making changes as you deem necessary) and tell him to initial each job when it's completed. Tell him the weekly chores on the bottom of the form need to be done only once before the week is finished. He can decide when to do those, or you can specify a day.

DAILY	*M*	*T*	*W*	*T*	*F*	*S*	*S*
Do Dishes							
Wipe Off and Put Away Appliances							
Wipe Off Table and Chairs							
Clean Countertop							
Clean Stove Top							
Wash Drip Pans							
Wipe Out Warm Oven (if used)							
Wipe Off Appliance Doors							
Dust Top of Refrigerator							
Sweep Floor							
Mop Floor, If Needed							
Empty Trash							
Clean Sink and Drain Trap							
Polish Fixtures							

An alternative is to put the initials of the person responsible in the appropriate box and have that person check it off when he's completed each assignment. In addition to this daily/weekly form, you may want to make one for monthly and semiannual jobs.

WEEKLY

Wipe Off Switches, Outlets		*Clean Phone*	
Wipe Off Doorknobs		*Remove Cobwebs*	
Wipe Off Cupbd. Doors, Handles		*Dust Shelves, Figurines, Wall Decorations*	
Wipe Off Windowsills		*Dust Door Ledges*	
Clean Vents		*Dust Hanging Lights*	
Clean Canisters		*Spot Wash Walls*	
Wash Sink Window		*Mop Floors, Baseboards*	
Wash Sliding Glass Door		*Wipe Off Shelves & Drawers Where Crumbs Have Accum.*	
Clean Range Hood			
		Clean Microwave	

Schedules see to it that a job isn't neglected longer than it should be, which only increases the amount of time it takes to do it. Schedules also prevent you from wasting time doing things more often than necessary. With a written schedule you never have to make the decision, "What should I do next?" Aside from that, a written schedule lists in black and white exactly what needs to be done so everyone can help. With a physical list, even a drop-in visitor would know what to do. The whole purpose of a schedule is to help you get the most out of what time, energy and money you have available—vital issues in today's busy world.

When determining your schedule, approach it with a questioning attitude:

Is this job necessary? If so, why?

Can I do the job in another way, another time, in another order, or in some other place?

Is it important that *I* do the job, or that the job just gets done?

Is the job appropriate?

Will it influence habits?

Will it make our memories happier or unhappier?

Will it spoil the aesthetic appeal of our home?

Does the job have to be done, or is it just a habit?

Now that we've prevented the need for so many tedious chores and scheduled the rest, all that's left is step number three: *do!*

GET IT DONE!

While I hardly, if ever, feel like Mary Poppins when I'm chiseling burnt-on food and grease from the bottom of the electric frying pan, I've learned that a spoonful of sugar does, indeed, help the medicine go down. Here are a few sweet morsels that help me, at least, tolerate kitchen cleanup.

Play some snappy music while you're puttering around in the kitchen. A nice fast piece helps you move along at a steady rhythmic pace. At any rate, have something pleasant going on. ("Read" a classic by means of your cassette tape player, have a special dessert baking in the oven, or visit with a friend.) The whole idea is to have a pleasant association with your work.

Break your jobs down into small, manageable portions, so the entire job won't seem so looming and unconquerable. For regular maintenance, divide the cleaning chores into fifteen- to twenty-minute segments every day, or devote some extra time one day a week. Or, after doing up the dishes, clean out one drawer or one shelf.

To thoroughly clean the kitchen, work in this order: cupboards, range, oven, fans, refrigerator, walls, woodwork, windows, sink, curtains (or window treatments) and floors.

Knowing the direction you're going to take makes breaking down the job much easier. If possible, plan a deep-cleaning session when your schedule isn't so demanding.

Categorize your kitchen chores into ABC priority. Some A's might be: dishes, countertop, empty trash. C's might include: wipe off doorknobs, dust top of refrigerator, clean canisters. That way if you're ever hit with a crisis (and who isn't from time to time) you'll know what the best use of your time is right now—the A's. The C's can wait, if they have to.

Keep cleaning supplies contained in a plastic cleanup caddy or other tote. Use it to hold your A-type cleaning solutions, a few soft rags, a Chore Girl and perhaps a plastic trash bag. With all cleaning supplies—be sure to take the necessary child-safety precautions. Remember, even if you don't have any young children, you may have children visiting from time to time.

For quick cleanups keep your cleaning solutions (neutral cleaner, nontoxic disinfectant, degreaser and evaporative alcohol-based cleaner) in spray bottles. Be sure you give the chemical a chance to work so you won't have to scrub. Let the solution penetrate and loosen hardened particles and all you'll have to do is wipe them away. (Again I'll refer you to Don Aslett's *Is There Life After Housework?* It's the uncontested winner for the "Fastest Cleanup This Side of China" award.)

HIDDEN DESTROYERS

One of the most important considerations in kitchen cleaning is to keep the kitchen from becoming a breeding ground for bacteria such as salmonella and e. Coli. There are three cardinal rules to follow:

1. Keep things clean.
   Wash your hands with soap or dishwashing liquid before you handle food.
   Wash pet dishes after animals eat. Their food gets contaminated, too. They can then transfer bacterial infections to the family.
   Clean cutting board, dishrags, sponges and dishtowels with a bleach solution to disinfect them. (Use 1 to 2 tbs. of bleach to a gallon of water.) These should be disinfected every time they come in contact with raw meat or poultry.
   Keep the refrigerator clean (wipe up spills immediately).
   Clean and sanitize garbage disposal, garbage pail and microwave oven frequently.
2. Avoid cross-contamination.
   Throw away any cutting board (whether wood or plastic) that is deeply scarred.

When you're in the grocery store, be sure all meats, fish and poultry are wrapped separately in plastic bags so they don't drip on other foods while they're transported home.

3. Cook and store food properly.

The refrigerator should be kept at 40°F or below. The freezer should be kept at 0°F or below.

Keep hot foods hot and cold foods cold.

Always carefully follow instructions when home canning or operating timed cooking or slow-cooking appliances.

While dirt and grime pose a threat to any kitchen, there's another more obvious type of pest to contend with: clutter. We tend to keep in sight what we want to keep in mind, so the clutter stacks up like cannonballs in a courtyard. And for some strange reason that "courtyard" is usually the kitchen. Coupons, canceled checks, credit card receipts, wrappers, bills, magazines, phone messages, check stubs, school papers and library books all accumulate. If the kitchen is the heart of the home and all this stuff is "pumped" into it, you could well be in the final stages of cardiac arrest. The following preventive measures will effect the "coronary bypass surgery" and rid your kitchen of clutter once and for all.

FAMILY ORGANIZER

The family organizer, described in detail in the book *Confessions of a Happily Organized Family*, is exactly what it claims to be. It's a loose-leaf notebook and contains a running telephone log (eliminating all those miscellaneous scraps of floating paper), weekly planning sheets for the kids, directory of frequently called phone numbers (and emergency numbers), sports rosters and schedules, school handbooks, and anything else the family needs to refer to on a regular basis. (Copies of the telephone log and the planning sheets can be found in *Confessions of a Happily Organized Family*.)

I demonstrate the family organizer at all my seminars and I've had to make up a "dummy" just for that purpose. You see, our family organizer has become such an important part of our family life, I can never remove it from home! It saves me at least two hours a week because we don't have to hunt for needed information, nor do we have to shuffle, stack and clean around the clutter. ("Clean around the clutter" is a sister slogan of "ring around the collar," I believe.)

PLANNING NOTEBOOK

For years I've been singing the praises of my planning notebook and, as promised, I'll sing again right now. Whatever floating paper is not obliterated by the family organizer is now put to rest here.

When I see a piece of paper, I decide if it's of general family interest or something that other members of the family will have to refer to. If so, it goes in the family organizer. If some of the details are necessary for me to be aware of, I copy them into my planning notebook (game times, work schedules, school information, etc.). When I receive notices from the PTA listing school days off, early dismissal times, holidays, activities, parent-teacher conferences, etc., I jot down the necessary information in the calendar section of my planning notebook and throw the original notice away. Ditto with wedding, shower and party invitations, appointment notices and anything else I'm notified about. The planning notebook, as you can see, has eliminated a lot of paper already—but there's more. I jot down reminders to myself about things I need to do—so my brain can relax and quit nagging— i.e., letters I have to answer, errands, articles to read, things to clean or fix, etc.

When I'm watching television or visiting with a friend and hear of a great new recipe to try—you guessed it—it's written in my planner. If I'm reading an article and discover something I want to send for, the address and other pertinent information is penned in my planning notebook.

My planner houses the shopping list; to-do's; incandescent, though rare, ideas; directions for getting places; book notes; meeting agendas; travel itineraries; car mileage; business expenses. In fact, all information that comes to me is recorded in a singular source, my planning notebook. For more information about the planning notebook, write to Home Management, P.O. Box 214, Cedar Rapids, IA 52406.

FILING SYSTEM—APPLIANCE RECORD

There's another type of paper problem consisting of incoming and outgoing mail, coupons, recipes, appliance manuals, receipts, check stubs and the like. Recipes and coupons were covered in chapters seven and eight, so let's zero in on the other stuff.

Every December I buy two expanding files for the upcoming year. One is letter size with twelve pockets (one for each month of the year) and another is made especially for cancelled checks. This is a very simple system, and makes filing so easy, it's a snap to keep up on it. Here's how it works. All cancelled checks, bank statements and deposit slips are filed by month in the check file. The receipts, paid bills, credit card purchase slips, etc., are filed in the large expanding envelope, also by month. If you ever have to refer to a receipt or check on a credit card purchase, you'll only have a handful of papers to flip through in order to find the one you need. This is much better than setting up a file for each company you do business with, because it eliminates confusion and wasted time. At the end of the year, pull your tax working papers, close up the files and keep them stored in a box for a few years. It's fast, easy and takes up very little room. I also recommend having one spot (say a decorative basket, dishpan or drawer) where all incoming paper is put until it is worked through the system.

It is also wise to keep track of instruction booklets, warranties and service information on the appliances you purchase. Here are two methods to store such information.

I have another letter-sized expanding file with several alphabetized pockets. The refrigerator booklet, receipt, warranty, etc., are simply put in the "R" pocket. The mixer information is placed under M, and so on. I usually keep the instruction booklet right by the appliance until I'm comfortable with and knowledgeable about its operation. Then, the booklet is filed away. This file is used for things in every room of the house (i.e., the kids' record player = R, piano = P, grill = G, care instructions for draperies = D). I don't waste time alphabetizing any farther than the first letter.

Here's the second method: Each appliance's information is placed in separate vinyl sheet protectors (sack type) and placed alphabetically in a loose-leaf notebook. (Or, you can use zipper closing plastic bags.)

If you're moving and going to leave any appliances in the house, be thoughtful and leave the instruction booklets and any other pertinent information for the new owners.

Appliance	Amount Paid	Check Number	Purchase Date	Where Purchased	Model	Serial Number	Service Information	Warranty Period

Errand Drawer

Where do you put things like this: the neighbor boy's Matchbox car, the cassette you borrowed from Marge, the agenda you need to photocopy, the cake plate that belongs to your neighbor, and the broken drawer pull you have to match when you buy a new one? The only logical solution is to pile them up somewhere (usually in the kitchen) so you'll remember to take care of all these little things.

Here's what I do. I make a note in my planning notebook to take care of whatever it is (or I delegate the chore) and put all the paraphernalia into the errand drawer. I'm not going to forget it because it's on my to-do list, but at least it's out of sight and not cluttering my kitchen. If you don't have a drawer to spare, use a cardboard box, tote bag or Rubbermaid stacking shelf (the ones with drawers are especially practical). Consolidate and conceal this junk and see what it does for your kitchen.

Landing/Launch Pads

These are simply in-out baskets for the kids. When they come home from school, all the debris is tossed in their respective dishpans. Articles they're clipping, books they're reading, lunch money, signed permission slips, etc., are all put into the landing pads. The pans launch them to school the next day with no hassles and no clutter piled club-sandwich-style on the kitchen counter. Cull the deadwood occasionally (corrected spelling tests, old math work, scraps from art projects) to keep the system running smoothly. You need one container for each child—tote or book bags, stacking bins, drawers, cardboard boxes, dishpans and baskets are all good choices. The best place to keep these containers is where the after-school rubble normally lands; that usually means in the kitchen. Stack bins in a corner or on a closet floor; hang tote bags from a peg; eliminate a few more C's from your kitchen to open up some shelf space. Wherever you keep them, landing and launch pads will make an arresting improvement in the appearance of your kitchen.

Toolbox

Every self-respecting kitchen needs a toolbox. Knobs on pan lids will loosen, as well as drawer pulls and door knobs. Decorative objects need to be hung from time to time (a few of them,

Plastic stacking bins are useful
anywhere you need extra storage.

though, have hit the ground so many times they are no longer
decorative). If your kitchen is the hub around which your house
revolves, then a toolbox will prove quite handy.

Here's a basic list of things to include: claw hammer, Phillips
screwdrivers (one large, one small), flathead screwdrivers (one
large, one small), pliers, utility knife, tape measure, tacks, masking tape, wire, hooks and an assortment of nails, wood screws,
nuts and bolts. Optional items: tack hammer, duct tape, nail set,
pipe wrenches, saw, level, sandpaper. Your tools can be stored in
a cardboard box, cleaning caddy, tote bag, drawer, crock, basket
or a small plastic toolbox. Mark each tool so you'll recognize it as
belonging in the kitchen. These tools will likely wander because
they'll probably be the only ones people can find with any regu-
larity. So don't allow them to be removed from the kitchen. (Since
not allowing people to do something doesn't usually work, mark
the gear so you can at least reclaim it.)

Junk Drawer

Over the years I've written about a lot of home management
problems, but I get more flak over the crummy junk drawer than
anything else. What is a junk drawer? It's a place where you put
things you don't know what to do with. Just look at all that stuff:

Batteries—the last time you used your tape player, Beverly
Sills sounded more like Tennessee Ernie Ford. So you bought
fresh batteries. These old ones were thrown in the junk drawer

because they still had a little juice in them. Or, you bought a four-pack and only needed two, so the extras were tossed in the drawer. Why not recycle those slow-motion batteries immediately and store the new ones by the appliance they'll be used with?

And what about the rope, tangles of wire, broken sunglasses, buttons, paper clips, unspooled cassette tape (as soon as you have a few minutes you're going to rewind it, right?), unidentified keys, rawhide bones and unused aluminum foil? Designate the junk drawer as a mini office center (for pens, pencils, stapler, staples, scissors, scratch pad, eraser, paper clips, tacks, tape, etc.); then CCC it.

Tools or hardware-type things go in the tool box. Buttons go with mending equipment. Things you've "been gonna" fix for over a year are discarded. If you have several fix-its in the junk drawer, make a note in your planner to fix each item, and store the projects in a box (and don't keep the box in the kitchen). Now that you know about prioritizing and storing at the point of first use, the junk drawer will be easier to dismantle.

Phones

If you have a cordless phone, you know what a blessing it is to be able to talk and continue what you were doing—whether it's folding laundry or weeding the garden. If you don't have one, and don't want one, purchase the longest telephone cord you can find. My superwoman friend, Sherrill, even scrubs her floor while talking on the phone. As a matter of fact, she's the one who converted me. Whenever I talk to her, she's doing something—washing dishes, watering plants, sealing her ceramic tile countertop. Only a cordless phone or a phone with a long phone cord will allow you to talk and work at the same time. Buy a shoulder cradle or self-adhesive phone cushion wherever phones are sold. That'll make the talk/work combination more comfortable.

Dishes? Toss 'em in the Trash

Even in kitchens with dishwashers there are always dishes piled in the sink, sprinkled across the countertop, stacked on the table or piled on top of any horizontal surface. The problem is that often the dishwasher is filled with clean dishes, and besides, no red-blooded American kid is going to take the time to check out whether the dishes are clean or dirty. Here's a solution, whether you have a dishwasher or not.

Keep a tall plastic wastebasket or restaurant-sized dishpan under the sink. When a dish is used, teach everyone to scrape and rinse it off and place it in the wastebasket. When it's time to wash the dishes or load the dishwasher, just empty the wastebasket and begin. Using this method your kitchen will always look fairly neat. Just be sure the dishes are done at least once a day!

If you don't have room under your sink, here's a decorative idea: purchase a pretty wicker clothes hamper with a lid and buy a plastic wastebasket to fit inside. The hamper can be anywhere, yet it'll conceal the dishes (or trash) you're keeping inside it.

To cut down on the number of cups and glasses you need to wash, here's a great hint. Buy a large, colored mug, cup or glass for each member of the family. (Each person gets a different color.) During the day, whenever anyone wants to drink something he uses his own mug instead of reaching into the cupboard for a clean glass. Perhaps you can keep the mugs in a dishpan under the sink or on a folded towel in the cupboard. After each use, just rinse them out and put them back. Or, hang the mugs on hooks inside the sink cupboard door. Once a day, mugs are washed with hot, soapy water. This one idea alone has been a tremendous time and clutter saver!

NITTY-GRITTY NOTES

- Divide cupboards into three, four or five sections and clean one section a day (or every other day). By the end of a week (or two) the cupboards are clean.
- Instead of regular shelf paper, try using freezer wrap. The tear-off box makes it easy to dispense just the right length. Also, there are many brands of rubber matting available to use as shelf liner. These work very well and keep drawer dividers from sliding around in a drawer.
- For cupboards not flush with the ceiling, cover the tops with plastic wrap, foil or freezer wrap. It can't be seen and will keep you from having to clean off greasy buildup.
- If you have kitchen carpeting, attach a small bag to the vacuum to hold the stray buttons, coins, toys, pins, etc., you discover while vacuuming. I also put things in the bag that

my vacuum won't pick up: dried palm fronds, wrappers stuck to the carpet and big chunks of anything.

- A small whisk broom hung on the vacuum is handy to use in corners or small crevices the vacuum head can't reach.
- An old toothbrush helps you clean between and around appliance buttons, can-opener parts, faucets, tines of forks, graters and strainers.
- A percolator brush is useful to clean the crumbs from the toaster (unplug the toaster first!).
- Before cleaning appliances, always refer to the manufacturer's instruction manual. If no booklet is available, check the nameplate on the appliance to determine the model number (or simply take a picture of the appliance). Send this information to the manufacturer along with your request for a new manual. If you don't have the manufacturer's address, call your local appliance dealer. He or she can give it to you.
- A long-handled windshield brush is perfect for retrieving stray pieces of food from underneath the stove or refrigerator and also reaches between large appliances.
- Secure a damp sponge (or old stocking) to the end of a yardstick to swish under appliances or to dust hard-to-reach refrigerator coils. (Unplug first.)
- Soak-and-dissolve is still the easiest way, but a plastic windshield ice scraper is good for prying loose dried-on foods from the floor, table or counter, if you're impatient.
- An old, but clean, mascara brush or a percolator brush is great for cleaning window tracks.
- Whenever you wash something (floors, counters, appliances), always rinse and buff dry, even if the product says, "No rinsing necessary."
- Clean out the refrigerator on garbage collection day if you have no food disposer (or freeze the unwanted food until garbage day). That way, you'll eliminate smelly trash and discourage neighborhood pets.
- Sponges, plastic scrubbers and dish mops will be clean and fresh-smelling if you occasionally clean them on the top rack of the dishwasher.
- Before broiling, put a few cups of water in the bottom of the broiler pan. You won't believe how easy it'll be to clean.
- To clean oven racks, spread a bath towel in the bathtub,

place the racks on top and cover with hot water. Add ammo-
nia and let soak.

- When mixing juice, Kool-Aid, etc., or when pouring anything, do it in the sink (or cover the counter with a paper
  towel or freezer wrap).
- Store small amounts of leftovers in microwave-safe paper
  cups. They're good for heating leftovers in the microwave
  without dirtying dishes.
- A lockable, portable metal file box is a good clean-up caddy
  for families with young children.
- Molded plastic high chairs are easy to clean in the shower.
  Remove any fabric pads, then spray on the hot water. Give
  it a chance to penetrate and loosen the cement-like globs,
  then wash clean and dry.
- Spread newspapers down under the high chair or under a
  small child's chair before every meal.
- To keep pet dishes in place, put a rubber jar ring underneath
  or use a baby suction-cup cereal dish. Or keep a placemat,
  towel or bathroom mat under the dishes to catch drips.
- A hanging purse file provides hanging storage for phone
  books, file folders, paper bags, boxes of wraps and foil, incoming and outgoing mail, magazines, etc.
- Do you have slits in your vinyl kitchen chairs? Cover them
  with bathtub appliques.
- Seal ceramic tile countertops once a year with Red Devil
  Tile and Grout Sealer. Simply follow the manufacturer's
  directions.
- When you want the kitchen to smell like you've been home
  all day working feverishly (and you haven't), put some orange peelings in a 350° oven.

In your fight against grime, keep your eye out for dust catchers
and dirt carriers and eliminate work at the outset. Be objective
and view your kitchen as a visitor would. What looks unkempt,
cluttered, dirty or worn out? Make a list and work on trouble
spots one at a time. Before long your kitchen will be a place of
refuge, not a place for refuse!

Chapter Ten

Entertaining With Ease

T here are those who think a party is not worth throwing unless it's done right: twinkle lights in the trees; three forks (and as many spoons) per place setting; tablecloths, china, flowers, hostess gown carefully coordinated with the color of the wallcoverings; the tinkle of a baby grand piano—all the while giving careful attention to every nuance of taste and texture of the catered fare.

Folks who run in those circles are not the audience I'm meaning to help. I'm after those who would just like to find time to entertain a few friends without throwing their backs out. Never mind if your house is thick with dust and thin on amenities, or you wince at the thought of your lackluster recipe collection. The most important ingredient for a successful party, besides a congenial group of people, is a list.

We all know someone who can throw a great bash with seemingly little effort. Her house might be as crowded as the Santa Monica freeway at 5 P.M., yet she mingles among her guests with the grace and unhurried poise of Vanna White demonstrating prizes on "Wheel of Fortune."

How does she do it? Planning. The more casual and effortless it seems, the more planning has usually gone into it. Good planning eliminates last-minute problems, making the event more enjoyable for the hostess and her guests.

The first question you need to ask is, "How many?" The number of guests you plan to invite influences the other things you need to consider (type of party, budget, etc.). If you're going to invite six people, a sit-down dinner is feasible. A group of twenty-five, however, might be better served by a buffet, cocktail party or an outdoor barbecue, for example.

Once you've arrived at a figure, think about the following:

- How much money do you want to spend? Again, this will have a bearing on the type of party you choose.
- Are you planning a party for a special occasion (birthday, housewarming, holiday) or is it just a get-together?
- Will your house comfortably accommodate this many people? How much activity will your kitchen (ovens, refrigerator, etc.) handle?
- Do you have enough place settings, tables, chairs and linens for a group this large? If not, what will you need to rent or borrow? Will rental fees fit into your budget?
- If you have children, where will they be, or how will they be cared for?

Once you've digested this information you're ready to do some hard-core planning:

- Who will be invited?
- Date and time of party?
- Type of party?
- What will be on the menu?

On the next page you'll find a copy of a party planner. If you don't have time to forget anything, write everything down on the form. After the event, put the completed copy in an entertainment file, which makes short work of future party-planning sessions.

The party planner is your schedule of events and constant reminder before the party actually starts. At the top of the sheet, jot down the number of guests, type of party and date in the appropriate spaces. Then, as you plan the menu, jot down each item in the menu section. (When the dish is actually completed, put a check mark by it.)

As you list each food item, jot down all the equipment you'll need for its service. Do you have an ovenproof dish that's big enough? Is there plenty of room in your refrigerator for all those salads? Portable toaster ovens, Crockpots, electric fry pans and microwaves can expand your oven space, and insulated ice chests can keep several small items cold. Perhaps a neighbor will let you store some of the overflow in her refrigerator or heat something in her oven.

PARTY PLANNER

Date _____ No. of Guests _____ Type of Party _____
Menu:

—— ————————————————   —— ————————————————
—— ————————————————   —— ————————————————
—— ————————————————   —— ————————————————
—— ————————————————   —— ————————————————
—— ————————————————   —— ————————————————

Equipment	Shopping List	Amount
—— ————————	—— ————————————	
—— ————————	—— ————————————	
—— ————————	—— ————————————	
—— ————————	—— ————————————	
—— ————————	—— ————————————	
—— ————————	—— ————————————	
—— ————————	—— ————————————	
—— ————————	—— ————————————	
—— ————————	—— ————————————	
—— ————————	—— ————————————	
Miscellaneous To Do	—— ————————————	
—— ————————	—— ————————————	
—— ————————	—— ————————————	
—— ————————	—— ————————————	
—— ————————	—— ————————————	

Next, list all the necessary ingredients and the amounts needed to make each dish. If the equipment or food is on hand, put a check mark by it. If not, the unchecked items will remind you that they need to be taken care of. Anything you need to purchase (ice, candles, special napkins, coasters, etc.) should be placed on the list.

On the bottom of the form is a section entitled "Miscellaneous To-Do's." Here you list such things as: pick up blouse from cleaner's, make appointment for manicure, hire baby-sitter, borrow Marcia's card table, pick up game prizes, order flowers, etc.

Now, post the party planner in a convenient spot or keep it in your planning notebook. Whenever a thought strikes, jot it down on your planner so it won't be forgotten and come back to haunt you later on.

TWO WEEKS BEFORE EVENT

Ten days to two weeks before the get-together, invite your guests in writing or just give them a call. During hectic holiday seasons, three to four weeks' notice is better.

Whether the invitation is oral or written, be sure to include the address and directions to your home (or the party location), type of party, dress, time and date. Even if you put RSVP on the invitations, you'll probably have to call a few people who forgot to let you know if they're coming.

Remember, though, that spur-of-the-moment parties are often the most fun of all. But even these require a little forethought.

Other things to do ten to fourteen days before: fill out the party planner; hire a baby-sitter and/or other help; order any specialties—flowers, deli, bakery, butcher, beverages, decorations; reserve anything you need to rent or borrow (chairs, tables, chafing dishes, snack sets, etc.); polish silver and wash seldom-used glassware and china.

PRE-PARTY CLEANING

Unfortunately, throwing a party usually includes housecleaning, so that chore needs to be scheduled as well. But there are a few tricks I've learned from expert party-givers that keep cleaning to a minimum.

One such expert is a professional housekeeper. She says the most important places to spruce up are: mirrors, any glass (light fixtures, mirrors, visible windows) and cobwebs. She maintains that sparkling glass and dust-free ceilings make the house appear clean, especially at night.

Another expert takes this approach: "Forget cleaning! Oh sure, you have to vacuum and straighten things up a bit and have at least one bathroom livable, but turn off the lights and use a lot of candles. Then, save your cleaning for after the party. More than likely, it'll need it!" She's right. Candles mask a lot of dust, fingerprints and water spots. Besides, everyone looks much better in candlelight.

I have a friend who is a wonderful entertainer and she thoroughly cleans only the rooms where guests will likely be. All other rooms are darkened and their doors closed. Her house is so attractive, people frequently ask her to show them every room. (That's what scares the rest of us!) But, my friend is a pro. She just laughs and says, "Are you kidding? I wouldn't let you into those awful rooms if you had a note from St. Peter!"

We went to a party one night and there was a colorful wide ribbon and bow in front of the stairs, which let everyone know (in a very nice way) that the upstairs was off limits.

Another effective way to get the most from a cleaning session is to have two parties back to back. You not only clean once and celebrate twice, you can double up on food preparation, decorations, equipment, etc., and save all the get-ready and cleanup of two separate affairs.

Some of you might have been swayed by a few of the above ideas. But, if you're like me, you're going to fear that someone will snag her pantyhose and snoop around in the bathroom for a bottle of clear nail polish to stop the run. Or (and it never fails) one of the kids will scamper into the living room and ask one of the guests if she'd like to see her bedroom. Or, someone will comment on your lovely antique buffet while innocently opening one of the doors, which reveals your single-sock collection, extra notebook paper, three unfinished projects, a shredded catnip mouse and a sweatshirt you shoved in there when the doorbell rang.

So, if you must clean, do down-under stuff (straightening drawers, closets, vacuuming under furniture, washing windows, dusting the blinds) days before the party and maintain your efforts until party time. Then, when you have a little free time on party day, dust and vacuum where needed, clean bathrooms, and check flowers, pillows and candles, and tend to other last-minute, light jobs.

CULINARY ARTS

Whether your party is a spur-of-the-moment fling or a seriously premeditated affair, you need to take special precautions when planning your menu, especially when time is of the essence.

I have a good friend who is a professional caterer. She has four basic menu plans she normally offers (though she will fill special requests). I think that's a great policy to incorporate at home, too.

With standard menus you become very proficient at making the dishes, you know the approximate cost (in terms of time and money), you know what can be made ahead, and since they're tried and true, you have a pretty good idea that the guests will enjoy the entrees. (However, if you entertain the same people frequently, you'll need more than four standard menus.)

In any event, develop a few specialties. Choose recipes that can be made a day ahead (or way ahead and frozen), so you won't have to do a lot of cooking on the day of the party. When planning your menu, choose something you've made before so you won't be surprised by a last-minute flop. If you don't currently have any specialties, pore over some cookbooks and try lots of new ideas. Pretty soon you'll hit upon a few good recipes you can always rely on.

Plan your main course first and additional courses around that. Keep all the food simple and complementary. Choose food that waits well in case guests arrive late. Don't be afraid to serve commercially prepared foods in addition to those that are home-made. Keep in mind, too, any guest preferences you're aware of (Emily is a vegetarian, Jean is allergic to nuts, Jim is on a diet).

Does the season or occasion suggest a menu? International fare is perfect for a bon voyage party. Football season is a good "kick-off" for a tailgate-style picnic; early spring is a nice time for a brunch, since it gives you a chance to make good the social obligations you've been collecting all winter.

How about asking guests to furnish part of the meal? Specify appetizer, dessert, salad, rolls, etc. Today, with everyone's busy time schedules, no one seems to mind taking over some of the food assignments.

Another way to get out from under food preparation time is to make fixing dinner part of the entertainment. This works especially well when there are not too many guests. Have one guest chop, another fry, another toss a salad and so on. Or, plan a meal (such as a stir-fry or fondue) that can be prepared right at the table. Buffets where you make your own sundaes, design an omelet or assemble a hero are tasty, fun and easy on the hostess.

Pick up food from a favorite restaurant; my favorite foods are Chinese and Mexican food because they reheat quickly. The deli is a great source for cheeses, salads and luncheon meats. They also fix nice platters that save you hours of chopping, slicing and coring. Top these off with a luscious dessert (homemade or purchased), and you've got a no-hassle winner.

Occasionally we have everyone meet at our house for appetizers. Then we choose a restaurant for dinner. Then it's back to our house for dessert and some frivolity.

Before or after any event (ballet, theater, sporting event, etc.) is an ideal time for a get-together. This type of entertaining lends itself well to appetizers or dessert service only—a real time-saver. Some of my favorite parties, by the way, are ones where only appetizers and desserts are served.

MANAGING THE BIG MEAL

What if you've decided on serving a big meal? Then, more than ever, it's important to follow the rules for general maintenance you read earlier in the book. Fill the sink or a dishpan with hot, sudsy water. Spread a sheet of freezer wrap or newspaper on the kitchen counter. Set out a handy trash container near your working center. This clean-as-you-go process gets you out of the kitchen faster than any other single thing you do, especially when you're working on a big meal.

SET A TIMETABLE

The following is a time plan for scheduling big meals so everything is ready at the same time. The time plan also helps you serve hot foods hot and cold foods cold. If it's done correctly, the kitchen will be presentable, too.

These time plans are extremely helpful when you're serving a multicourse meal and they're good practice for beginning cooks who want to polish their culinary skills. With experience, everyday meals do not require the precision of a written time-table, but even though I have years of cooking experience under my belt (literally and figuratively) I always use a time plan for the really big, important meals.

Here's what you do. First, check the party planner. Be sure you've listed the complete menu and all nonfood jobs. Also decide what can be done a day or more ahead, and schedule it on your calendar or note it on the party planner.

Here are some good jobs to do ahead: set the table, crisp the fresh vegetables and salad greens, arrange relish trays, make stuffing (but don't stuff poultry until just before cooking), butter French bread and wrap in foil, whip topping, make dips and salad dressings, measure water and salt for cooking frozen vegetables, potatoes or rice, set salads, make rolls and dessert. Serving tables and dishes can be set out a few days before the party if you're pressed for time.

To keep made-ahead sandwiches fresh, place a damp towel in the bottom of a shallow pan. The edges of the towel should hang over the sides of the pan. Place waxed paper over the damp cloth and stack sandwiches in the pan, putting wax paper between each layer of sandwiches. After placing a final layer of waxed paper on the top of the sandwiches, fold the towel over them.

Now it's time to fill out the timetable. Draw up a columnar chart as illustrated on page 163. Allow one column for every dish in your menu plan. Any last-minute nonfood jobs you listed on the party planner (light the candles, spot-check the house, turn on the stereo) can be put into one category (final cleanup check).

As you can see from the illustration, each dish in the menu is listed at the bottom of each column. Times are listed in ten-minute increments in the far left-hand vertical column, ending with the time the dinner is scheduled to begin.

What food will require the longest preparation time? Let's say your menu plans call for homemade crescent rolls, which you estimate will take 2½ hours. If you're serving dinner at 7:30, then you must start the rolls no later than 5:00, right? Better yet, start them at 4:30. It's always smart to allow yourself a little extra time so you'll have a cushion for cleaning as you go and for any unplanned interruptions.

Dish	4:40	4:50	5:00	5:10	5:20	5:30	5:40	5:50	6:00	6:10	6:20	6:30	6:40	6:50	7:00	7:10	7:20	7:30
Stroganoff Mix, Cook												■	■	■	■	■	■	■
Wild Rice Prep & Cook															■	■	■	■
Peas & Onions Cook																	■	■
Salad—Do-Ahead																		
Crescent Rolls	■	■						■							■	■	■	
Choc. Chip Cake—Do Ahead																		
Beverage Mix—Pour																■		
Set Table									■	■								
Final Cleanup Check															■	■	■	■

In the crescent roll column, then, darken the spaces between 4:30 and 4:50. These twenty minutes will be used to mix and knead the dough. The dough will rise between 4:50 and 5:40 and will not require any attention, so leave those spaces blank. From 5:40 to 5:50 the dough will be rolled, cut and set to rise again. Darken the 5:40 to 5:50 area. The rolls will need no further tending until 7:00, when you bake them. Darken 7:00 to 7:20. Continue in this manner, filling in preparation times for each item on the menu.

You'll notice at the end of the chart there's a ten-minute time cushion for last-minute checks. Finish tidying up the kitchen. If you've been cleaning as you go, this won't be much of a job. Double-check the table and set out anything that will not be affected by room temperature for ten to twenty minutes or so. Recheck your party planner to make sure you have set out all the food. More than once I've discovered a wonderful (but forgotten) salad when I'm putting things away after dinner. And finally, check the bathrooms to be sure the towels are still fresh and to wipe up any drips.

The timetable gives you a very visual method of tracking your predinner schedule. Of course, you could just make a list indicating what time each job needs to be done. Either way, you'll be able to serve good food on time in tidy surroundings.

FOLLOW-UP AND FILE

After the guests go home, or the next day, spend a few minutes completing the follow-up form. Actually, you can start filling out this form as soon as you decide to have a party. Use it in conjunction with the party planner, filling in the date, place, theme or occasion, decorations and guests. After the party, fill in the remainder of the form.

Under "comments," record any impressions you had about the success of the party. What would you do differently? What seemed to work well? Here is where you might say: "No one commented on the cranberry salad and there was a lot left over." Or, "Everyone loved the cheese roll."

The entertainment section is where you jot down what games you played (and the response) or if you used professional entertainment. Note who, what and how much it cost.

Guest information is especially helpful when planning future

FOLLOW-UP

PARTY DATE: _____

PLACE: _____

SPECIAL OCCASION OR THEME: _____

DECORATIONS: _____

_____

Guests:

WHAT I WORE: _____

Hired help: Who, what for, cost, comments:

ENOUGH FOOD? ____ ENOUGH/PROPER EQUIPMENT? ____

ENTERTAINMENT: _____

_____

_____

_____

Comments:

Guest Information:

events. I record things like this. "Roberta doesn't like sweet and sour." "Rick loves cherry pie." "Dan and Steve don't get along too well." "Ann's favorite flavor is burnt almond fudge." "Yvonne admired my handmade doilies."

Here's how I put this information to good use. We keep our name and address list in a Rolodex file. With each person listed on a separate card, there's plenty of room to jot down useful information.

On the back of Roberta's card, let's say, I either make a note about the sweet and sour or write the date of the party, which will refer me to the entertainment file. Note: I staple the party planner, the follow-up sheet and the timetable (if I used one) together and put them chronologically in the entertainment file. The next time I invite Roberta to a party, I check the back of her card and it leads me to the party planner that refers to her.

These notes not only help me to be a more thoughtful hostess, but when Yvonne's birthday comes up, she'll be awfully surprised when she receives a pretty lace doily.

I keep track of a lot of things: names of friends' and relatives' children, upcoming trips or other special events, hospital stays, favorite colors or flowers—anything that someday might help me say, "I care about you."

In addition, the party planner and follow-up sheets help to plan future parties. In the future you can invite different people and have the exact party all over again. Most of the planning will already be done.

TIPS FOR A HEARTY PARTY

- After cleaning the house for the last time before the party, if you need to feed the kids, cut out the front of a big cardboard box and put it on the floor in front of the TV. Serve the kids right in the carton. It keeps crumbs off the floor and fascinates the kids. (Or keep them occupied in the box working on a craft.)
- A baby-sitter can take the children out for hamburgers and a movie and bring them home and put them to bed. Or, have the sitter baby-sit in the children's rooms.
- When fixing the refreshments, pack a small box or bag of goodies for each child and send it with them when they go

to their rooms (or into the far reaches to watch a video).

- Put a signal on your house so guests will be able to spot it more easily. (Tie a bow around your mailbox, display a colorful banner, paint a message on poster board using luminous paint.)
- When using place cards at a sit-down dinner, be sure to write the guests' names on both sides of the card. That way if the visitors are not well acquainted, they'll know to whom they are speaking during dinner.
- If you're expecting a big crowd and you have only a small house, serve food in different rooms. Set up tables and chairs anywhere there's available space or serve the appetizers in the living room, salads in the kitchen, main dishes in the den, etc. This keeps the crowd moving and mingling, yet no one area will be overly congested.
- Use an ice bucket for serving food. Because it's insulated it keeps things either hot or cold.
- Dried fruits arranged on a platter are great appetizers. They require no preparation, they're delicious, and they are ready and waiting for guests who arrive at any time.
- When serving sandwiches, cut them in different ways to serve as a code. (Diagonally cut sandwiches have mayonnaise, horizontally cut have mustard.)
- Use your automatic coffeemaker to steep cider, cinnamon sticks, cloves and allspice. (The spices go in the coffee basket.) Brew as usual.
- For a one-of-a-kind tablecloth, use a white sheet and let your guests sign it using a permanent laundry marker. Use the same cloth at all your parties, so the guest list keeps growing.
- A bread-and-butter party is easy and inexpensive, not to mention good-tasting. Serve a wide assortment of breads and flavored butters. If you want to, add an array of cheese, cold meat, raw vegetables and fruits.
- Have a snack-luck party. Everyone brings their favorite snack. You provide the beverages. Or, have a simple buffet where you serve mugs of soup, salads, rolls and dessert.
- Start up a lending co-op with your close friends. Everyone lists the things they've got plenty of and would be willing to share (snack sets, folding chairs, card tables, chafing dishes).

Type up a list and circulate it among the members of the group.
- Next time you have a bridal shower, tell everyone to bring some household goods they no longer use or want (in addition to a new gift). It's a great way to get rid of things and help out the new bride at the same time.
- Pack leftovers in decorated doggie bags and give to your friends when they leave the party.

If you'd like to feel like a guest at your own party, try some of these ideas. Even if you quail at the thought of having a party, even if your house is more like a hovel, there's a party you can give with a flourish.

HELPFUL HINTS FOR SPECIAL OCCASIONS

Christmas is without a doubt the biggest season, requiring the most planning and preparation, so we've devoted a whole chapter to it (chapter eleven). But the rest of the year is no picnic. There seems to be no end to occasions calling for your talents and time. Again, be creative and have fun with them. Here are some ideas.

When You're the Guest

- For a nice hostess gift, bring your favorite appetizer. It will definitely be appreciated!
- Bringing punch to a party? Pour a few inches into a clean milk carton and freeze it. Refrigerate the rest. When it's time to go, pour the cold punch over the frozen. The solid layer will keep the beverage cold and won't dilute the mixture.

Easter

- Making Easter cookies? Cut egg-shaped cookies, sprinkle with colored sugar and bake. They come out speckled—just like real bird eggs.

Charitable Giving

- Nursing homes and hospitals are swamped with generous offers during holidays (especially Easter, Thanksgiving and Christmas). Why not schedule your organization's visit and gifts for another time of the year? Your attention may be more appreciated then and everyone in your group won't be quite so busy.

Welcome Party

- Welcome new neighbors with a pounding party. Everyone brings a pound of staple food (flour, sugar, rice, etc.) on move-in day. Treat the new family to a casserole or dessert, and don't forget the paper plates, cups and plastic forks.

Be Prepared

- Buy a few sets of soaps, jams, candles or herbal teas. Take them apart and use as token gifts for unexpected guests or as an "extra touch" to a prepared gift.

SPICE UP EVERYDAY MEALS

Making occasions festive is one thing, but putting some fun into everyday routine takes a little extra effort. Try some of these ideas, the effort is worth it—your family will enjoy them and you will too.

- For a special (no extra time) touch at dinner, fill a brandy snifter with crisp, raw vegetables. Sprinkle crushed ice on top.
- One evening a month, serve a foreign specialty and set the table accordingly. Try Mexican night with tacos and green and orange place mats, or Chinese night with egg Foo Young and fortune cookies. Don't forget about Italian, German, Norwegian and Indian.
- When serving the family beef stew, chili, a one-dish casserole or other "cowboy grub," use bandannas as napkins, pie pans for dishes, and small Mason jars for glasses.
- Make quick centerpieces with what you already have on hand: shiny apples look great piled in a wicker basket or wooden bowl, or core them and use them for candle holders—then have baked apples for dessert. Drop limes, cherry tomatoes, nuts or pinecones in a glass jar or bowl or an airy woven basket.
- If you can't afford to take the whole family out for dinner but want to enjoy a meal out once in a while, eat breakfast

out instead. Breakfast meals are cheaper (and usually faster).
- For a nice touch at breakfast, why not provide room service to the children or your spouse? A continental breakfast of juice, sweet rolls and/or toast and hot chocolate is easy, yet it conveys your special thoughts.

ESPECIALLY FOR KIDS

- Send a hostess gift when your child sleeps or eats at a friend's house—juice, cookies, popsicles. It's a nice way to teach your child about gratitude.
- For a child whose birthday comes in the dead of winter (especially those around Christmas) how about having a half-birthday party? One year my sister decided to have one for her son, whose birthday is December 24. For invitations, she made and frosted a batch of cupcakes and cut each one in half from top to bottom. Then she used extra frosting to mount each cupcake to small pieces of poster board on which was printed the half-birthday invitation. Each edible invitation was then hand delivered. For the first time Michael had a summer birthday and enjoyed warm weather events. (It's a much better time of year to get a new bike, too.)
- Make edible place cards by writing the child's name with icing on a sugar cookie.
- For a birthday party activity, have each child decorate his own birthday cake. Bake one for each child using a small round cake pan from a play set. Be sure the pan is ovenproof, though, before you use it.
- For an easy special touch, mold gelatin in clean plastic toys (horse head shovel, cars, castles, clay molds, etc.) or festive cookie cutters.
- Fill ice-cream cones with tuna, egg or chicken salad, cottage cheese or yogurt.
- Plan a picnic for the kids. All invitees bring their own lunch. You provide the blankets, punch and dessert.
- On days when the kids are baking (as long as you're going to have a mess anyway) why not invite one of their friends? Choose someone who needs cheering up or could use a little extra attention (such as a child whose parents are divorcing

or a new child in the neighborhood). One year we invited a Japanese boy who had just arrived in the United States and couldn't speak English. It's nice to include a child who just needs a friend, but old friends are fine, too. Entertaining is about giving, after all, and everyone likes receiving!

Once you've absorbed this bit of education, you can move on to your entertaining doctorate. Let the ideas in this chapter serve as a springboard for your own ingenuity and you'll discover that entertaining is an enjoyable part of life—for guests and hosts alike.

Chapter Eleven

Have Yourself an Organized Christmas

S omeday I'd like to meet Mrs. Clement Clarke Moore. Her husband, you recall, wrote: "'Twas the night before Christmas when all through the house, not a creature was stirring, not even a mouse."

Imagine, not a creature stirring on Christmas Eve! Mrs. Moore, with her donned kerchief and settled brains (another amazing Christmas Eve feat), was not exactly dressed for success, yet somehow she managed to hang the stockings with care by the chimney, nestle her children all snug in their beds, and still have time for a long winter's nap! Amazing.

One year the Christmas season was so frantic around our house, I wrote myself a letter (after the fact) outlining the gory details. Here are a few highlights:

Dec. 12: Searched rain gutter for Christmas tree lights. Still there, but not in good shape after a year of outdoor storage.

Dec. 14: Jeffrey wrote a letter to Santa Claus saying, "It isn't fair to leave presents for only good kids."

Dec. 17: Kids made and decorated sugar cookies to give to their friends. Since we had only one rolling pin, it seemed natural that any dough needing to be flattend be sat upon. Flour stuck like hard paste to the counters, table and floor. Colored sprinkles and a rainbow of Christmas-colored icings dribbled down chair, table and human legs, only to dry as if caught in a moment of suspended animation. With the aid of a putty knife, two aspirins and a lot of "Bah-Humbugs," the kitchen was temporarily put back in order.

Dec. 18: Delivered sugar cookies to kids' friends after visiting the convalescent center, rehearsing for the Christmas play, taking a case of canned goods to the sub-for-Santa site; but before the junior high choir concert, the office party and the trip downtown to see the lights.

Dec. 20: Spent most of the day doing Christmas cards.

Dec. 21: Christmas baking for my friends.

Dec. 22: Christmas baking for my friends. Hated every minute of this baking session. Had more important things to do, but a strong sense of obligation kept me going. Couldn't just say, "Thanks," when friends shoved baskets and tins full of home-made goodies into my arms. Hated cookies, nutbreads and candy. Hated friends.

Dec. 23: Delivered baked goods to friends. Went to Erma's. She asked if I'd just made the cookies. Said, "Yes." Asked how she knew. Erma pointed to the two flour handprints on my back-side (which I always find more convenient than a hand towel). Hated Erma. Later that night turned Christmas carolers away empty-handed. All the baked treats had been given away. Didn't make any for our family.

Dec. 24: Hunched over unwrapped presents with hands on knees as though losing a bout with indigestion. Used all the news-paper and comics. Wrapped rest of presents in brown paper bags. Smeared a lot of camouflage stick under my eyes.

Many times during the next year I reread my letter, using it as motivation to organize and enjoy future holidays. The trick worked!

Whether you want to celebrate a child's grand slam home run or capture the spirit of the holidays, keep reading. If you pay close attention, you'll not only pick up a lot of time-saving ideas, you'll be able to enjoy any celebration with more gusto!

PLAN, PLAN, PLAN

Right about now you're probably thinking that I sound like a broken record. But unplanned expenditures of time will ruin things. Take a few minutes early in the season (or before any upcoming special event) to begin planning your activities. I usu-ally start serious holiday planning during the summer. Of course, some plans for next year's Christmas are conceived this Christmas. Casual planning could begin as late as September or October. Waiting until Thanksgiving, though, is going to be too late. List gifts to make, gifts to buy, cards to be purchased and addressed, baking, mailing gifts and cards, making decorations, buying the tree, decorating the house—whatever you can think of.

Write these plans down. When you have a tangible list to look at you can use your physical senses as well as your mental processes. It's impossible to organize, prioritize and pare down a mental note. So, write down everything you can think of that needs to be done—even if you know you won't be able to do it all. File your plans—it'll make things much easier next year.

Talk to school teachers early in the school year to find out about holiday activities. Will there be after-school rehearsals, evening performances, special costumes required or anything else you can plan for?

If you're a serious holiday celebrator, set aside a holiday section in your planning notebook where you record gift ideas, plans for the upcoming event, gift and card lists and so forth. (If you don't use a planner, simply record the information on the back of next December's calendar.) That way you can cash in on sales all year long and eliminate some of the last-minute frenzy. Also, include in this section the layouts of your favorite department stores:

Nelson's Dept. Store:
First Floor: cosmetics, shoes, purses, accessories, stationery, books.
Second Floor: clothing—men, women, children.

Call your chamber of commerce and ask what your town has planned for the holidays. Schedule those chosen activites on your calendar so you can plan ahead and work around them.

Whenever possible, use the layaway services of a large department store. If you purchase all (or a majority) of your gifts in one store, you'll have your shopping done in a few hours; and using layaway means you don't need cash in hand (though a deposit is usually required). Another benefit is that you don't have to hide them from the kids—and no storage space is needed. Laying things away forces you to plan ahead so you can shop before the crowds frazzle your nerves and limit your selection. Also, for gifts going out of town, many stores will ship them for you. When all our children were little we frequently bought our gifts in a local department store. Everything was put on layaway in late October. In December, we picked up the gifts and the store wrapped them for free!

Meal planning will save hours of time. Even if you never do

it otherwise, do it now, at least. Select simple meals so you can serve hot, nourishing food during the hectic weeks coming up. Start dinner and baking after breakfast so you can have one cleanup. From Halloween until Christmas, bake and freeze varieties of cookies so you can have a large assortment ready without much hassle.

Now that you have some plans and ideas scribbled down, look over the list and check off only those things you feel are especially important, and schedule them in your calendar. Roughly prioritize the rest of the list and schedule as many things as you can realistically handle. One of the best ways to save time and escape from the kitchen is to take the emphasis off food—particularly as gifts. (Some specific ideas follow.)

Cut back as much as possible. Everyone will enjoy the season much more if they're not under so much pressure.

Must you have a Christmas party? Why not schedule a party for some other time of the year? Or have a holiday get-together between Christmas and New Year's? There's sometimes a lull in people's schedule during that week.

Instead of sending a newsy Christmas letter, why not do it on Valentine's Day? One of my friends does this every year and the results have been surprising. She used to send the letters at Christmas but decided it just added to her usual holiday frustrations. So, one year she typed up her letter and mailed it to close friends and relatives on Valentine's Day. It was such a hit with everyone (because everyone else had more time to enjoy it), she's continued the practice.

Another friend enjoyed making homemade food gifts but, as always, time was too hard to come by after Thanksgiving. Now she delivers her gifts just before Thanksgiving with a lovely card expressing her gratitude for good friends and wishing them a happy holiday season. Isn't that a great idea? It accomplishes the purpose of the holiday season; it's more thoughtful (less obligatory), less hurried and probably more appreciated by the receiver.

A neighborhood basket is a wonderful time-saver. Here's how it worked in one neighborhood we lived in. One family filled a basket with special treats and passed the basket on to the family next door. The basket was refilled and passed along from house to house. It was a good way to say, "Happy Holidays" to each other without fixing individual gifts.

I love homemade gifts—crafts as well as food—and I like to share them with friends and especially my family. But handwork, particularly, is so time-consuming (and my family is so large) it seemed impossible to whip something up for everyone. Frustrated by a dearth of ideas (what should I give the neighbors *this* year?), a lack of time, yet a desire to create, I started making what I call Christmas Idea Boxes.

As soon as Christmas is over I start making simple little projects (decorations, ornaments, nonseasonal house decorations), or I buy them at those wonderful after-Christmas sales. These are usually portable projects and I never walk out of the house without something to do. So, most of the crafts are assembled during waiting or transportation time, during ball games or while watching TV.

Then in July or early August I assemble the idea boxes, putting a few of the finished projects in each (along with the instructions). I write a letter to each recipient saying that I'm sending their gifts early enough so they can, in turn, make some for their friends and relatives. So, I'm not only sending a gift, but ideas they can use, which become very precious when holiday crunch time comes around.

This has been so much fun. All year long I feel the warm spirit of giving, yet I'm actually spending less time than I was before. Because I've planned early and used up snatches of time I would have otherwise wasted, my holidays are much less stressful. I have more time for holiday baking, sleigh rides, snowball fights and enjoying (rather than loathing) the season.

Don't Forget the Kids

Holidays can be stressful for children, too. The anticipation and excitement of the season sometimes turns even the most docile child into what would best be described as a cheerleading super action hero. I remember how much I enjoyed Christmas night when the children were little. They were finally calmed down after six weeks of near pandemonium. Some psychologists recommend alleviating some of the tension by giving the child a few token or trinket gifts occasionally before Christmas.

So, I made an Advent calendar with twenty-four pockets in it. Inside each pocket I place a piece of paper on which is written the location of a hidden treat. These daily presents are simple things like: a pencil, comb, gum, cereal box trinkets (collect and save them during the year), a holiday cookie, balloons, stickers, an afternoon of making gingerbread houses or building a snow fort, a trip to see a special display of Christmas lights and the like. This has proven to be one of our favorite traditions and has helped the kids cope with the anxiety and helped me experience peace on earth, good will towards children.

TIME-WISE GIFT IDEAS

Here are some gift ideas for and from the kitchen that take little time, but they're thoughtful, considerate and a refreshing change from traditional holiday treats.

One year we received one cookie and candy tray after another, and naturally we gratefully gobbled down every last piece. But by the time Christmas was over we were so sick of sweets we could hardly face another bonbon or piece of toffee. That's when I decided we should give fruit instead of candy, cakes and cookies. (The truth is, I stopped giving candy because as a candy-maker I make a great bricklayer. As our kids always say after I make fudge, "This tastes great, Mom. It's *hard*, but it's good!")

During the year, collect inexpensive baskets and then in early December fill them with fruit: oranges, apples, grapefruit, pine-apple, kiwi, etc., whatever is plentiful. Wrapped in cellophane (clear or colored) and topped with a bow, these fruit baskets are well received by everyone and more appreciated now that we're all increasingly health and diet conscious. In one hour (including

Inexpensive baskets can be collected during the year, and filled with fruit in early December.

shopping time) you can have a counter full of gift baskets ready. A counter full of homemade things would have taken all day. You can still include homemade treats in the basket—and this will give you more time in which to make those goodies!

In addition to the common sources, thrift stores, garage sales and flea markets are wonderful places to find inexpensive, un-usual or one-of-a-kind containers in which to pack your gift, be it homemade or purchased food, or a useful tool.

Remember, your food goodies do not have to be homemade to be appreciated. If you're uncomfortable with that, try putting a purchased food treat in an unusual or practical container. For some reason, it restores your feeling of pride.

Some good containers to look for: bottles, baskets, wooden bowls, wineglasses, brandy snifters, beakers, crocks, pitchers (small and large), jugs, bowls, mugs, canisters, trays, beanpots, glazed pottery, casseroles, scoops, dessert molds, soufflé dishes, mixing bowls, pans (all types), oven mitts, ice buckets, cookie tins, flour sifters, nut choppers, muffin pans, porcelain teacups and salt and pepper shakers. (The teacups and shakers are espe-cially nice for collectors.)

The nicest gifts (and the most memorable) are those that are personalized. Below are some tips to get you going, but add some of your own. If you know someone who quilts, make a quilter's gift selection; or if you have a friend that skis, collect goggles, lip balm, ski wax and other essentials and package them up in an appealing way. Now here are some more ideas to get your creativ-ity flowing.

- Give fresh herbs growing in tiny clay pots. Or, present dried herbs in ceramic canisters, small decorative tins or any pretty container.
- Pour seasoned oil, vinegar or salad dressings into cruets or one-of-a-kind bottles. Top with a cork and tie a pretty rib-bon around the neck.
- Give some seasoned salt in a new shaker. Or how about giving a pepper mill and a can of peppercorns?
- Put hot cocoa mix or gourmet coffee in a large colorful mug or other creative container.
- Wrap up a package of wooden skewers with a gift of olives or pickles.

- Heap colorful produce (tomatoes, peppers, fruit) in a brass, graniteware, or other decorative colander.
- Coverall aprons are always nice to receive. If you like, tuck a few kitchen tools or food treats inside the apron pockets.
- For the omelet connoisseur, give a flexible spatula, herbs and a favorite omelet recipe. Or give the recipe for cherries jubilee with a half-gallon of vanilla ice cream. Fancy pasta is the perfect accompaniment to your minestrone recipe. For a main dish, put the directions and a key ingredient in a new casserole dish.
- Give a favorite recipe as a gift and include one of the ingredients (gingersnaps with a sauerbraten recipe, walnuts for sugared walnuts, cinnamon sticks with a mulled cider recipe). Put a box of gelatin inside a copper mold and include the recipe for a delicious set salad or dessert. Pour cornmeal into a novel container, add a recipe for corn bread and tie on a wooden spoon.
- Collect a few favorite recipes from the recipient's friends and relatives and give her the collection in a card file or notebook. (Be sure to include the name of the donor on each recipe.) Or, fill a notebook or card file with your own favorite recipes.
- Fill a tote bag with small kitchen gadgets (peeler, apple corer, bottle stoppers, tongs, melon baller, skewers, measuring spoons, spatulas, etc.). Tie something to a wire whisk, ladle or large wooden spoon.
- Cents-off coupons for products your friend uses are a practical gift idea. Fill a basket with canned goods or cleaning supplies and tuck the coupons inside.
- If you want to spend hours putting faces on gingerbread men, that's fine. But if time is working against you, these are nice and easy foods to give: berries, fruits, jams, jellies, honey, cheese spreads, flavored butters, salted or spiced nuts, nuts in the shell, popcorn, popcorn balls, caramel corn, candy, dried fruit, citron and purchased bakery products.
- Also, think about things everyone needs and frequently runs out of: paper towels, dishcloths and towels, candles (tie a bunch of tapers together with a bright ribbon or raffia), bag of charcoal, stamps, recipe cards, batteries, glasses, ice-cream dishes, fireplace logs, paper plates and cups, plastic

tableware, immersion coil, ice-cream scoop (box it up and include some Baskin-Robbins or Dairy Queen coupons), hand lotion, memo pads (Post-it notes are great), herb seeds or gift certificates.

- Find some odd saucers and fit each with a fat candle in white or harmonize with the saucer's color.
- How about a new cookbook? Write an inscription on the inside cover and put a star by each of your favorite recipes. A serious cook would likely appreciate a subscription to *Gourmet* magazine (or something similar).
- One year my sister Judy gave us a big popcorn bucket. She purchased a large metal bucket, spray-painted the outside and attached several decals. She also got eight tin cups and decorated them to match. (All in all, this was a thirty-minute job.) To finish the gift, she included a two-pound bag of unpopped popcorn. That bucket served us faithfully for many years. It was practical, cute and not time-costly.
- Give a gift of candy in an apothecary jar, ice-cube tray, desk organizer or kitchen drawer divider.
- A brandy snifter displays and contains a selection of hard candies, spiced nuts, jelly beans or whatever.
- Canisters for flour and sugar are nice for cookies, nuts, popcorn, caramel corn, crackers or pretzels.
- Deep, large scoops are creative containers for candies, gourmet popcorn (unpopped), doughnut holes, jelly beans or whatever. Fill and cover with plastic wrap or cellophane, then add a festive bow.
- For kids on your list, fill up a toy with cookies and/or candy. Good choices are plastic boats and dump trucks, lunch boxes, bicycle baskets, sandpails and any toy with a hollow space large enough to accommodate the treat.
- Fill different-sized mason jars with Christmas candy, wrap the lids with colorful calico and tie with yarn, ribbon or raffia. Set the bottles on tables, mantles, windowsills, etc., to use as party decorations. When your guests go home, give each one a jar of candy.
- Hang gingerbread men from houseplants, house trees or mantles and give to carolers and other guests.
- Give a cake mix wrapped in a new cake pan. Include a box or can of frosting and a decorating tool.

- Give a purchased or homemade cake on a new baking pan. Put cookies on a shiny new cookie sheet or in an ice bucket.
- Steam a pudding or bake a bundt cake in a new pan and give it as a present.
- Fill a punch bowl, salad bowl, colander or bread box with doughnuts, sweet rolls, bread or popcorn.
- Put a colorful kitchen hand towel in a basket and fill with muffins, bagels or cookies.
- Present bread on a cutting board. Pack cheese spread, flavored butter or cream cheese, or canape spreads in a pâté mold, ramekin, crock or ceramic jar, and attach a spreader.
- Wrap a gift of bread (homemade or bakery) in a festive dish towel—or one that matches the recipient's kitchen—and tie with ribbon, raffia or yarn.
- A person who lives alone would enjoy a selection of frozen home-cooked dinners in single-serving size. Top it off with a beverage, rolls and minidesserts.
- Decorate some lunch bags or paper tote bags. This is a fun project to do with the kids. You can write "Treats from Trixi's Kitchen" or write your friend's name on a whole stack. They're cute and creative as gift containers. Use rubber stamps, magic markers, finger paints, glitter, felt, holly, ribbon or anything festive. Or, have a bunch printed up at the local printer.
- Instead of tying a bow on top of your kitchen-related gift, why not attach a plastic scrubber or sponge?
- To inexpensively package any homemade treat, save TV dinner trays and fill with an assortment of things. Or, if you never buy TV dinners, Styrofoam trays are available at any butcher or the bakery department of the store for just a few cents each. They, too, are handy for containing your homemade foods. (They're also good for transporting food when you have to bring a dessert to the church social, for example. You don't have to worry about getting your dish back.) You can also save the aluminum foil pans that come with store-bought coffee cake or bread.

The whole idea is to be inventive. You'll be amazed to discover how much time you can save just thinking things through. Don't be afraid to do something different. It's much more fun for you and a pleasant surprise for the recipients!

This chapter has more ideas than the patent office, so you're left with no excuses. This year, before you get involved in an all-night wrapping session, stop for a moment. Promise yourself that once and for all you will have peace on earth at your house. Plan well, prepare early, and on Christmas Eve not a creature will stir.

Chapter Twelve

Kitchen Design Ideas

I s there a kitchen counter revolution in your future? Are your planning guerrilla warfare with a "take no prisoners" approach, hiring a crew large enough to man the Vatican guard, and overseeing the removal of planet-sized chunks from your existing kitchen? Great!

Even though it's a messy job, it can be exciting and fun from the first planning steps to the first load of dishes you wash in your new kitchen. Everyone enjoys a new kitchen for many, many years and if it's done right, a good kitchen will increase the value of your home.

However, maybe you're thinking more of a "coup" than a revolution: a few cosmetic changes, a couple of added conveniences—maybe things Cousin Egbert could do on Saturday afternoons.

No matter your approach or what the desired result, there are some important things to consider before you begin.

PLAN FIRST

Even before you begin perusing magazines, kitchen design catalogs and model home interiors, you need to begin thinking about your life-style, your desired life-style, and your particular needs. Knowing these things in advance will help your kitchen designer, architect or handyman give you exactly what you want and need.

To get you started, here is a Life-style Questionnaire. Jot down the answers so you'll have something tangible to work with. Star the items most important to you. That way if it's impossible to get everything you want, your designer will at least know your priorities.

1. Did you want a major overhaul or just a new face? Are you

just bored with your old kitchen or is it seriously dysfunctional?

Generally speaking, if your kitchen is newer than ten years old, a retouch is probably all you need—unless, of course, serious structural problems are causing time or space difficulties.

Maybe new countertops, flooring, cupboard doors or appliances would be enough to perk things up. There are many specialty shops that refinish existing cabinets, replace cupboard fronts or install plastic laminate surfaces that can update a drab look. New fluorescent lighting does wonders for kitchen work areas.

But if you're ready for a knock-down-drag-out fight, here's what to plan for.

While a major renovation is going on, the kitchen will be closed. You will need to remove and pack up everything—food, utensils, dishes, pans, etc. Pack, label and stack cartons containing B- and C-type goods, leaving only the A's for daily use while you camp out in another room (or on the deck or patio).

Here's a tip for packing up the things you won't be using for a while. Take a carton and write "#1" on each side of the box. Then on a sheet of paper put "#1" in the upper right-hand corner. List on the paper all the items you put into the box. When the box is full, close it up and start box number two and a new sheet of paper labeled "#2" and so on. In the event you need something in the interim just scan your lists and you'll see immediately which carton contains the needed item.

Cooking can be accomplished by means of small electric appliances, charocal grill, immersion coil, hot plate, fry pan, Crockpot, camp stove and microwave. If possible—or if necessary—move the refrigerator to the new campsite. Dishes can be washed in the bathroom, garage or laundry area. You may also want to include some extra fast-food or restaurant meal expenses in your kitchen planning budget.

Also, the water, gas and electricity may have to be turned off from time to time while the workmen execute their chores. If possible, get a written time estimate from your contractor (including time, date and length of turnoff). The day before a scheduled turnoff, recheck with your contractor to make sure the schedule is still on track.

Also, a full-blown attack on the kitchen is going to raise a lot of dust that will settle in even the nether areas of the house.

Cover furniture with sheets, plastic or drop cloths. Take any necessary precautions with carpeting or flooring you want to protect.

2. Set limits for your time and money budgets. Decide how much you will spend on your renovations and how long you are willing to be unsettled and living in dust. Your contractor should know exactly at the outset what you're expecting from him or her.

For example, it would be fair to allow six weeks (maximum) to live in the dust and chaos, and maybe an additional two or three weeks you could tolerate having some of the finer details left undone. We'll talk about finding and working with a quality crew in a minute.

3. What do you like about your existing kitchen? Be specific. "I like the cupboards that go clear up to the ceiling. The pantry is well located. The long narrow cupboard is perfect for the toaster."

4. What do you dislike about your kitchen now? "The dishwasher is too far from the sink. The dark countertops show every crumb. The floor is dull and colorless. When we're fixing dinner, everyone gets in each other's way. I'm bothered by the street noise and the blare of the TV."

Notice the number of steps you take when you're preparing something. Do you stretch or bend continually? Make a note of these annoyances. Also consider things like the placement of the telephone and nearby storage for pens and paper.

Is there a passing traffic pattern going through kitchen work areas? Can you see into the kitchen from the front door? (My pet peeve.) Is the kitchen visible when sitting in other rooms of the house? If these things bother you, write them down on your gripe list.

Pay strict attention to detail here because even the tiniest problem may pose a terrible inconvenience yet might be correctable. Case in point: When you walk into our kitchen and flip on the light switch, the backyard patio light goes on. In order to illuminate the kitchen, you have to grope and stumble, feeling your way across the room until you reach the switch (which, by the way, is next to the backyard patio). It was a small oversight that has proven to be a big pain.

5. What is your cooking style? How many people usually cook at once? How many people are involved in cleaning up?

What kind of a cook are you—gourmet, vegetarian, family-style?

Roll-out bins are handy for
vegetables.

Do you do a lot of canning, dehydrating, freezing and baking? How
about cake decorating or candy making? Do you do a lot of outdoor
cooking? If so, you'll need direct access to the yard. What are your
most common specialties? Your kitchen designer should be aware
of any A- or B-type activities.

Do you have any specialty tools, appliances or other equipment? What priority (ABC) are they? Priorities of awkward-sized
equipment, especially, should be made known to your kitchen
planner.

How tall is the person who does most of the cooking? A 36-
inch counter height is standard, but can easily be adjusted up or
down—varied for comfort. (Extremes in countertop height may
affect the resale of your home, so you want to carefully consider
this option.)

What types of things do you keep in your drawers? Or what
types of things would you like to keep in your drawers? Trays,

bread, files, bins for flour, sugar, potatoes and onions?

Are you concerned with appearances, or is convenience your byword? If the latter is "you," then hanging pans and utensils, open shelves, wall-mounted dish drainers and glass cupboard doors might be suggested. However, if everything has to be picture perfect in your kitchen, you'll have to plan plenty of undercover storage spots.

Do you want cupboards that go clear to the ceiling (providing good C-type storage on the top shelf) or do you like the decorative look of a soffit? Do you want to eliminate the soffit and display collectibles on top of your cupboards?

Do you need to utilize every square inch of space or do you have plenty of room? If space is limited, you might want to think about having stick-built (custom-made) cupboards rather than buying stock ones. The stock cupboards will probably not fit your space exactly and spacers will have to be used between units. However, custom-made cabinetry will be built exactly to your existing space specifications.

6. Now, list the other types of things that go on in your kitchen. Do you mend, wash and dry clothes, read, play games, watch TV, listen to music, participate in crafts and hobbies? Do the kids use the kitchen as a homework center? Is your kitchen a mail room, as well? Do you want these activities to go on in your new kitchen or will some be moved to another area of the house?

At this point, be realistic and honest with yourself. You may very well decide that nary a scrap of mail will ever be placed in your new kitchen. But seriously, a year from now, after the newness has worn off, can you see yourself enforcing the new rule? If not, plan now for a mail center (or whatever) so you won't be faced with the same problems presented by your old kitchen.

7. What have you always wanted in your kitchen? A desk, the laundry equipment, a family room, indoor barbecue, a baking center, a deep freeze, a bumpout window seat, a rocking chair, a fireplace? Go for it. Remember, right now all we're doing is planning and dreaming. Once you have a roughly written worksheet, you can prioritize, budget and eliminate.

8. What is your eating style? Do you have three meals a day, sit-down family dinners, or is it "every man for himself" during the day and one sit-down meal at night? How many people (maximum) will you want to serve at a sit-down dinner? Do you like

to eat in the kitchen or would you prefer a formal dining room (or both)? My favorite arrangement is a large kitchen with a snack bar for breakfast, lunch and snacks, a table for family dinners and a separate dining room for special occasions.

Do you entertain often? Do you prefer formal or casual entertaining? Do you like people to visit with you in the kitchen while you cook, or do you, like Greta Garbo, want to be left alone?

Your plans should be firming up nicely by now. While you're going through these questions, though, think generally about any foreseen future needs. Are you just beginning your family, or is your family starting to leave the nest? Will grandchildren be visiting frequently? Are you planning to live in this house for a while or is a move looming in the distant future? As you progress up the corporate ladder, will you be called upon to entertain clients in your home? Do you want your children to bring their friends home for pizza and ice cream after the movies? Be sure to think about your life-style in present and future tenses.

Now that you've scribbled down a few thoughts, rewrite a neat listing of your wants and don't wants. Then, make two copies— one for you and one for your kitchen planner. Check off or star the things most important so you won't mistakenly axe a great idea.

Be sure you've written purposes, not solutions, on your list.

Slant shelves make it easier to rotate your food supply.

Pull-out base cupboard shelves look like three drawers when closed.

For example: "Need more storage for canned goods" is a purpose. "Build slant shelves for canned goods" is a solution. Listing the purpose will enable you to consider many options, allowing you to choose more objectively the *best* solution.

Now it's time to peruse those magazines, kitchen design catalogs and model home interiors. Get a file folder and fill it with pictures of anything that strikes your fancy. (Take a camera along with you when you visit showrooms, model homes and stores. Put the developed snapshots into your remodeling file.) This file of information will give your kitchen planner a better idea of the look and specific features you're most interested in.

CHOOSING A DESIGNER/REMODELER

Now that you know where you're going with your kitchen, it's time to find an expert.

An expert, they say, is anyone who lives at least fifty miles away and has a set of 35mm slides. Since your kitchen is a major investment in the value of your home, it's important to find someone with better credentials than home movies. Just because a guy has the word *remodeling* painted on the side of his pickup truck doesn't necessarily mean you should turn over your kitchen to him.

What you're looking for is a professional who has a record of experience in the kitchen field. It is not out of line to find out how long the contractor in question has been doing business or to ask for referrals. I would be leery of anyone who doesn't have a showroom or an address listing in the phone book.

Find someone who is a designer and space planner, particularly if you're doing an in-depth renovation. The American Institute of Kitchen Dealers designates accredited kitchen representatives by the initials CKD (Certified Kitchen Dealers). They have passed exacting, qualifying tests to receive this accreditation. So, if it's possible, choose a CKD.

You might think if you have an architect, an interior designer and a contractor that you've got all you need, but then you have three separate entities with which to work. A CKD, however, can pull everything together. So, get a good CKD, then follow his or her recommendations for any additional help you might need.

Since remodeling is difficult at best, choose a designer who is easy for you to work with. If you have obvious personality conflicts before the project begins, imagine how problems will balloon midstream. If your kitchen planner is very assertive, for example, you may well end up with a kitchen the way *she* wants it instead of the way *you* want it. So, choose someone you feel comfortable with and can talk to easily.

Visit showrooms and get a general idea of prices, craftsmanship and quality grades. Talk to the salespeople and designers. With the knowledge you now have about kitchen efficiency you'll be able to discern which designers really know their stuff.

Once you've made your choice, the kitchen planner will visit your home, look over your kitchen and take measurements. A truly careful professional will never accept your measurements, no matter how intelligent you may be. So don't be offended.

Once he's sized up the situation, give him a copy of your Lifestyle Questionnaire and the file folder of pictures you've col-

A fliptop mini garage door keeps appliances out of sight, yet easy to reach.

lected. Point out exactly what it is you like about each of the pictures. Also, the planner might like to have a copy of your personalized centers' lists that show what you store in each of your work centers.

After careful consideration, the designer will meet with you again to present you with ideas and a bid. This proposal should include job description, price and terms of payment, approximate completion date, procedures for breaking the contract or making changes or corrections, cleanup responsibilities, and length and type of warranty.

As the construction date approaches, a few preliminary preparations will get things started quickly and smoothly. Take everything off kitchen walls and remove all decorations. Don't forget towel racks, hooks, wall-hung appliances (or appliances attached to any cupboard that will be replaced). Remove the contents from all the cupboards and drawers. Take down all window treatments and all window treatment brackets.

If there is furniture in your kitchen (bar stools, TV, bookshelf, table and chairs, etc.), get it out of the way before the work begins.

Clear a spot in the basement, garage or carport where building materials and new appliances can be stored when they're delivered. Planning now will help eliminate inconvenient disruptions later on.

If you're planning to do some (or all) of the work and designing yourself, get some good reference books. Time-Life Books and

Sunset Books have good planning and remodeling series. They are helpful, easy to understand and very visual guides.

APPLIANCES DESIGNED WITH TIME IN MIND

Conquering time is our challenge today and manufacturers are answering the call with efficient, time-saving and easy-to-care-for appliances. When considering the purchase of major appliances, get the most for your time and money by reviewing the following guidelines.

How much space is available? You may not have enough room for a double oven or a side-by-side refrigerator. Measure your spaces carefully.

What installation will be required? Will you have to change from a gas stove to an electric model, or add a water line for a refrigerator with an automatic ice-maker or cold water dispenser? How energy-efficient is the appliance you're considering? How much will it cost to operate it?

Buy a good brand that has a reputation for durability. Check *Consumer Reports* at your local library. Look up the product in the periodical guide to see if other magazine articles have been written. Get good information from unbiased sources.

How long do you expect to use the product? List the features you want and arrange them in priority order. Look over the owner's manuals before purchasing.

Shop around to discover the various models and styles available. If possible, talk to someone who owns a particular style

A pop-up appliance shelf keeps your small appliances out of sight, yet easy to use.

you're considering. I was thinking seriously about purchasing a stove top advertised as almost revolutionary. I spoke to a friend who had one and she talked me out of it in a hurry. She found it extremely difficult to clean and she pointed out that the burners were so close together she couldn't put two large pans on the stove at the same time. I decided against the purchase and have been very happy with a much simpler model.

A pull-out corner base cupboard eliminates dead space and puts everything in full view when opened.

Simplicity is the solution to a lot of problems. Some appliances nowadays will do everything but baby-sit. The more "gingerbread" you have tacked to your appliances, the more you increase proportionately the following: cost, chance of breakdown, repairs (costly in time and money) and cleaning around all the nooks and crannies.

Also in this same category are appliances built into the countertop. Aside from the above-mentioned objections, they also limit your versatility and available counter space.

There are, however, some bona fide time-saving features that are worth the extra monetary investment. My favorites are pull-out base cupboard shelves and adjustable upper shelves; self-cleaning oven; snap-out electric heating elements on stove top; time-bake oven set (put food in the oven, set the timer and the oven starts and stops automatically); self-defrosting refrigerator/freezer with adjustable shelves; automatic ice-makers; built-in (as opposed to portable) dishwashers; continuous feed garbage

Pull-out base shelves make everything easier to see and reach.

disposals; and textured appliance doors that disguise fingerprints.

Trash compactors are not included in this list of goodies. I have had more than one type of trash compactor and hated all of them. They need to be cleaned frequently and that can be a major undertaking. Often a piece of sturdy trash will become lodged between the wastebasket and the plunger, making it impossible to open the compactor door. There are, of course, millions of people who couldn't live without their trash compactors, but I'm not one of them. It's so much easier to use a tall plastic wastebasket with a plastic trash bag liner.

Basically, when weighing one model or feature against another, look for removable parts for easy cleaning, and adjustable shelves. Beware of carved, molded or severely textured surfaces that will increase cleanup time.

Read and understand the warranty. Buy the product from a reputable dealer who offers good, reliable service. At least, be sure that service centers for your particular appliance are readily available in your area. Also, ask about the appliance's expected life span.

A pull-out pantry or chef's cupboard is an extra worth splurging on.

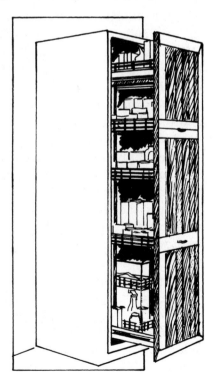

When checking the cost of the appliance, ask if there are any other costs you're not aware of, like delivery, installation, maintenance contracts or service charges. Find out what the dealer's return policy is, should you be dissatisfied. Check to see if the appliance is safety-tested by a certifying agency—Underwriter's Laboratories (UL), Association of Home Appliance Manufacturers (AHAM), American Gas Association Blue Star, for example.

Last, and certainly not least, when the appliance is delivered, take a few minutes to read the instruction manual. Using the appliance correctly will likely add years to its life. Keep the manual handy for periodic review until you're thoroughly familiar with the various functions of the product.

CUPBOARDS, COUNTERTOPS, FLOORS

You can save even more time by selecting easy-care and efficient building materials.

Cupboards made from wood, metal or plastic laminate are easier to clean if they have fewer trims, moldings and grooves. They are more functional when shelves are adjustable and base cupboard shelves pull out.

Unless you're naturally neat and orderly, have doors installed on your cupboards. Open shelves and glass doors not only keep everything in full view, but they can add to your cleaning time. Splashes, dust, grease splatters, etc., will settle on the shelves and their contents, or become obvious on glass doors. So think twice before choosing the "open" look.

Often shelves and drawer interiors are made from particleboard that has been oversprayed with a sealer. In time these surfaces swell and become rough to the touch. Also, cans, gadgets and pans mar the interior surface. The best alternative (albeit the most expensive) is to have shelves and drawers' interiors made from wood covered with plastic laminate. It's easy to clean, requires no shelf liner or painting and looks good for years.

Some good built-in features are slide-out garbage (and/or recycling) receptacles, bin drawers, spice cabinets or drawers, slide-out cutlery trays and chef's cupboards. Appliance "garages" hide appliances that provide convenient, yet concealed, countertop storage.

The main considerations when buying floor coverings are easy

A built-in spice rack installed in the front panel under the stove top provides one-motion storage.

care, comfort, price, durability and appearance. Today the run-away best-seller is the vinyl resilient floor. It's comfortable to stand on for long periods, easy to clean and requires only occasional waxing or polishing (even no-wax floors). It is pretty, affordable and does a good job or resisting grease and alkalis.

There are two basic types of vinyl: rotovinyl and inlaid. The rotovinyls have the pattern printed on the flooring. It's lighter in weight, which makes it easier for a do-it-yourselfer to install. The inlaid vinyl's pattern is built up in layers made from vinyl granules that are fused together. This type of floor is more substantial (and more expensive) than a rotovinyl floor, and because of its sturdy construction it's harder for a nonprofessional to install.

Each floor type can be purchased with a vinyl or urethane no-wax finish. The vinyl resists stains better, but the urethane is tougher and keeps its shine better. For a high-traffic area like a kitchen, I would recommend an inlaid vinyl with a urethane finish. Armstrong's Solarian and Mirabond are examples.

Glazed brick and ceramic tile are other popular choices. They are extremely attractive, very durable and keep their good looks for years. However, they're uncomfortable to stand on for long periods of time. Also, when a dish hits the floor you'll most likely be getting out the broom and dustpan.

Wood floors are very attractive. They're warm and durable and, when covered with a penetrating sealer, are even moisture resistant. They need to be refinished from time to time. Unless you're willing to pay a high maintenance price for the beauty of a wood floor, don't have one installed in your kitchen.

Kitchen carpeting is subject to much debate. You'll either love it or hate it with a vengeance. It's attractive, durable (and that's an understatement) and comfortable. But, things will spill, grease will splatter, and dogs and kids will come in from the rain. Most of the folks I've spoken to who are kitchen carpet advocates have small families with older kids or no children.

Whatever your choice, select a covering that's awash with color. Golds and yellows magnify dirt, and dark floors are especially hard to keep looking clean. Lighter shades (except stark white) are always preferred over dark.

When shopping for a countertop, look for the same features you'd want in a floor: easy care, durability, price, beauty, etc. Also, the same color guidelines apply (light colors are preferable to dark or white).

Plastic laminates are very popular (both smooth and textured). They are easy to clean and are heat-resistant (not heatproof), but they are subject to occasional cuts, stains and burns. When purchasing this type of countertop, choose one with a molded backsplash for ease in cleaning.

Ceramic tile is pretty durable, heatproof and stands up to cutting and chopping. It wipes up easily and individually damaged tiles can be replaced. Be sure the tile you choose has been fired for countertop use. If it's ceramic tile that is to be used on a floor, it will crack when something hot is set on it.

You may want to select a colored grout and always seal it. (Repeat the sealing procedure approximately once or twice a year.) On the down side, ceramic tile is noisy and dishes break more easily when dropped on the counter.

Wood or butcher-block counters require special treatment (sanding, oiling, disinfecting) to keep them looking good. I prefer using a separate cutting board that can be stored in less than perfect condition under cover.

Synthetic marble looks like marble but has added advantages:

it withstands heat, stains and cracks. Although it scratches easily, mars can be "erased" in effect by lightly sanding.

Metal counters or partial inserts are good for holding hot pans and bakeware. Metal does cut and scratch, however, so if you're leaning toward metal, choose a brushed satiny finish that will camouflage the eventual wear and tear.

Marble is another possibility. It can crack and stain, though, and because it's enormously expensive it would be a good choice to use as a separate countertop or partial insert for pastry and candy making. Granite is another option.

There are a myriad of choices for your countertops and floors. In this brief chapter, however, I've only attempted to discuss the most popular choices. For more information check with your kitchen planner, home center, department stores, builder, yellow pages, kitchen dealer or the books I referred to earlier.

DESIGN INTERVENTION

- The garbage disposal should be installed in the sink closest to the mixing center.
- The dishwasher should be to the right of the sink if you're right-handed. Reverse if you're left-handed.
- Some appliances come with removable colored panels so you can change your decorating scheme without replacing the whole appliance.
- Appliances can be repainted by a professional who specializes in electrostatic painting. In fact, this process is perfect for any metal surface—bookcases, file cabinets, metal kitchen cabinets, etc.
- If your kitchen is tiny, you will gain much-needed storage space by having ceiling-high cabinets installed.
- If your kitchen is open or visible from another room, be sure you coordinate the decorating schemes.
- An ordinary trellis, when painted to match your kitchen decor, can be attached to any vertical surface and used to hang gadgets, pans, etc., or to display collectibles. (Use S-hooks for hanging the equipment.)
- A decorative stepladder is handy as a plant stand when not being used for its intended purpose.
- Baskets are a great addition to any kitchen. Make an

attractive grouping to hang on the wall; fill sitting or suspended baskets with magazines, plants, potatoes, apples,
onions, pinecones, nuts, matchbook collection, cookie
cutters, dried flowers, etc.

- For a clever and appealing way to get extra counter space,
  stand an antique ironing board in a kitchen corner. Even
  placed out of the way, this is a perfect spot to cool freshly
  baked goods, to serve a buffet or to plan menus.
- Dispensers installed in the recesses between wall studs are
  handy for storing paper towels, bread, boxes of wraps and
  such. This arrangement frees up counter and drawer space.

In the seventeenth century Henry Kett voiced this warning to
all would-be builders and remodelers:

"Never build after you are five and forty; have five years' in-
come in hand before you lay a brick; and always calculate the
expense at double the estimate."

Though a kitchen renovation can be a David and Goliath con-
frontation, with the help of this chapter, you, too, can fell the
giant, even after you're forty-five!

CONCLUSION

Scrubbing Kitchen Myths

Nowadays everyone is working in the kitchen. The first one home often has to get things underway—whether it's a man, woman or child! Because it's everyone's kitchen, organization is the only answer to keeping things running smoothly. When everything has a well-defined place no one has to create a mess looking for things or putting things away.

But despite my best efforts, the "stuff still sticks to the sides of the pan" once in a while. It's during those times of self-pity and discouragement that I reflect upon a letter I received recently.

A woman wrote to tell me how much she appreciated many of the ideas she had read in one of my books. She was the mother of four children under seven. She enthusiastically explained how she hated cleaning her kitchen, but new ideas sparked her interest and actually made the job more enjoyable and easier for her.

She awoke every morning to a clean kitchen. Her husband kept commenting on how much better things looked and how the atmosphere at home had improved. She had more time to play with her kids and even found time to watch TV shows with them. Her recipes were organized and they were eating a wider variety of meals and spending less time preparing them.

Oh. I forgot to mention that this family has no running water. It's amazing, isn't it, that no matter what circumstances in which you find yourself, you can make things a little bit better.

Nowadays there are many CEOs who are also CCBWs (Chief Cook and Bottle Washers). No matter who we are, what we do, how many of us live together, we all have one thing in common— we don't have time. And what time we *do* have is usually spent hurrying.

Remember that quote I referred to in the beginning of the book? It said that if we are concerned about managing our time more effectively, we must choose the kitchen as a primary target for more efficient organization. That doesn't mean we have to give up great-tasting meals or other kitchen delights. All we have to sacrifice are a few bad habits that eat up time we could spend with the people and activities we love.

Don't be a slave to housework. If your dishrag is flying at half mast, hoist it clear up to the top of the pole and let freedom ring!

INDEX